TO:

_____

FROM:

_____

DATE:

_____

❀

True Stories of
True Love
from People
Like You

Dr. Rich Davis & Barnett Helzberg, Jr.

ADDAX
PUBLISHING
GROUP

Published by Addax Publishing Group, Inc.
Copyright © 2001 by Dr. Rich Davis and Barnett Helzberg, Jr.
Managing Editor: Matt Fulks
Designed by Laura Bolter

I AM LOVED® is a registered trademark of the
Shirley & Barnett Helzberg Foundation

For Information address:
Addax Publishing Group, Inc.
8643 Hauser Drive, Suite 235, Lenexa, KS 66215

ISBN: 1-58497-010-3

Printed in Canada

1 3 5 7 9 10 8 6 4 2

Library of Congress Cataloging-in-Publication Data

I am loved : true stories of true love from people like you / edited by
Rich Davis and Barnett Helzberg.
    p. cm.
  ISBN 1-58497-010-3 (pbk.)
  1. Love. I. Davis, Rich, 1926- II. Helzberg, Barnett, 1933-
  BF575.L8 I2 2001
  152.4'1—dc21
                                    00-065061

Dedication

All love starts at home and with family for those of us lucky enough to start life that way. Keeping love alive through life's stresses and conflicts is not always easy. So to my parents and brother, and my wife, children and grandchildren, I dedicate this book on love, with love. I do believe I Am Loved.
I know you are, too.

Richard, Dad, Gramps

For Shirley who inspired it all…
For our boys who multiplied it tenfold…
Love Always,

Dad

Acknowledgments

It is impossible to thank all of the wonderful people who helped us spread this great news of love, especially considering the large number of stories we received for consideration. However, we send our special thanks to the following people who were instrumental to the book's development: Dee Barwick, Len Boswell, Pola Firestone, Matt Fulks, John Goodman, John H. Graham IV, Brian Hakan, Charlie Kopke, Bob Snodgrass and Tom Viola.

We send our thanks to the many friends and acquaintances who contributed stories to this collection about the world's most precious commodity … LOVE.

True Stories of
True Love
from People
Like You

Introduction

The idea for this book came up spontaneously during a casual dinner Rich Davis was having at a café in Paris. A small group of couples gathered for early supper. During the conversation something prompted the telling of a "love story" between grandfather and grandson. This spurred others to share experiences that had similar emotional impacts on them. Then and there the idea for the book was born.

Knowing of the trademark "I Am Loved®" that Barnett Helzberg, Jr. had created, the two ideas seemed a natural pair! We got together and, hence, this "I Am Loved®" book. Little did we know when we started this project that the outpouring of stories would be so incredible.

The parameters for this book are quite simple ... each story is an example of when someone was on either the giving or the receiving end of love. Basically, these are shining examples of when people knew they were loved. Like love, these stories are powerful. It was difficult for us to read more than two or three stories before we'd each get a lump in our throat, a tear in our eye, or a smile on our face.

Webster's New World Dictionary defines love as a "strong affection or liking for someone or something." Doesn't love actually go deeper than that? Love can be defined or described in numerous ways. For instance, love can be considered random acts of kindness. As Arthel Neville, one of the book's storytellers, says, she spreads love through generic, simple acts of kindness to people she knows, as well as to strangers she passes on the street.

One of the first things you will notice in the upcoming pages is that unlike most books, there is no table of contents, only a list of contributors. Since love, unlike any other emotion and feeling, is random, the stories in this book have been placed in no particular order. Each story is special. Your favorite stories might be different from ours. Hence, no specific order. The majority of the following stories —about 99 percent— are original, written specifically for this book. We also have several pieces of "refrigerator art" from kids that parents and grandparents have saved through the years, and graciously sent to us for use in the book.

Another thing you will notice is the special blank pages at the end of the book. After you have read through these stories, you likely could be spurred to write your own "love story" to make this book more personal for you. The story you write will help make this book more of a keepsake, and will help you pass along your story to others. After all, love is best when it's shared. Throughout the book you will see our stories as well as one from our editor. After reading through the other stories, we felt compelled to share our stories of love.

Love is as pervasive and beautiful today as it always has been throughout history. Heaven knows it's more badly needed today than ever before. Once you have read this book, we hope that you, too, can truly say, "I am loved."

Rich Davis & Barnett Helzberg, Jr.

Contributors

Nate Accardo
William C. "Duke" Akers, Jr.
Wally "Famous" Amos
Thomas E. Beal
Robert F. Bennett
Becky Benson
Bert Berkley
Beth Bernard
Henry W. Bloch
Erma Bombeck
Dick Bond
Brad Bonney
Mrs. W. Coleman Branton
Michael Braude
Bobbi Bridge
Ruby Bright
Joanie Brody
Margaret Brown
Dick Clark
Dr. D. Kay Clawson
Jeffrey & Martha Comment
Bud Cooper
Tom Davidson
Rich Davis
Beverly Deming
Sheila Kemper Dietrich
E. Grey Dimond, M.D.
Julie Doherty
Patrice Eilts-Jobe
Arnold Eversull

Bonita Favre
Suzanne Fenton
Jerry Fladung
SuEllen Fried
Matt Fulks
Dewey Gaedcke
Jim Gerson
Anita B. Gorman
Jessica Graham
Patti Greene
Bud Greener
Bill Grigsby
Cliff Gruber
Debbie Hagen
Dot Hagman
Brian Hakan
Don Hall
Adele Hall
Linda Hall
Cheryl Hanback
Tod Haren
Kyle Harrison
Margaret Harsh
W. H. Helmerich III
Barnett Helzberg, Jr.
Conrad Hock
Kolin Holladay
Beth Ann Holzclaw
Joan King Holtzman
Kim Isenhower

Contributors

Joan Israelite
Andrew Jacobs
John M. Jenks
Renee Kidwell
Rick Krska
John L. Levy
Art Linkletter
Barbara Littman
Joan Lucas
Bobbi Marks
Ann McAdam
Ida McBeth
Harry McCray
John McMeel
Bev Menninger
Adrienne Mielke
Arthel Neville
Skip Nottberg
Cydney and Bill Osterman
Rosalie Sanara Petrouske
Jim Phillips
Nancy Poetz
H. Joseph Price, Jr.
Kathy Rainen
Elyse Rohrer
Susan Rohrer
Jessica Rudnick-Kaseff
Ken Samelson
Father Jim Savage
Thomas J. Savage, S.J.

George Schrader
Carl Schulkin
Dick Shaw
Jeanne Sheehy
Joan Shields
John H. Shore
Susanne Christopher Shutz
Bob & Betty Slegman
Stanley N. Stark, M.D.
Peter King Steinhaus
Betsy Stewart
Kathryn Callaway Sullivan
Bill Tammeus
Shelley Tauber
Ron Tutt
Helen Jane Uhlmann
Paul Uhlmann III
Jo Ann Ulrich
Barbara Unell
Rev. Charlann Walker
Janet Watson
Stu Weber
Joanna Wright
Rabbi Michael Zedek
Julie Zimmer
Matt Zimmermann

Call Me Mama

October 23, 1978 was one of the happiest days in my life. I was blessed with an 8-pound, 10-ounce baby boy exactly one month after my older sister had given birth to her son. My becoming a mother was a dream I never thought possible due to some health problems.

As the months passed after my baby was born, I became concerned because he wasn't progressing as rapidly as my sister's son was. My mother kept filling me with hope by saying all children develop in different stages and for me not to worry that my child had not spoken a single word even though he was now 2 1/2 years old.

My son was diagnosed with autism, a neurological disease that affects the central nervous system. Disruptive behavior and little or no speech are a couple of the many symptoms of autism. My daily prayer to God was, "Lord, if you just let me hear Jason call me mama (for some reason I believed if he could say mama he could say anything), I would be the happiest woman in the world." Time and life went on.

One day I was asked to perform on a cruise ship for four weeks. I hadn't left my child since his birth (at this time he was 5 years old) but decided the change would do me good to get away for a little while.

I was so home sick and missed my baby terribly. It seemed like I had been gone four years instead of four weeks. Flying back home felt like an eternity. When I finally arrived home, I ran inside calling and looking for my baby. He was at the dinner table, his face and hands covered with peanut butter & jelly. He looked up at me with those beautiful, dark brown eyes, smiled, and simply said, "Mama, mama," just as loud and plain as can be. I was so shocked and thrilled I just fell on my knees and kissed and hugged him, shouting out loud, "Thank you God! Thank you father!"

I can truly say that was, and still is, one of the happiest days in my entire life. Yes, I am loved.

Ida McBeth

❀

Aliene

April 28, 1996, my love would have been only one year younger than I, which was an amusing subject between the two of us. Our 55th Wedding Anniversary was to be November 20, 1996. We were unable to celebrate it.

In 1993, my wife, Aliene, was diagnosed with A.L.S., a.k.a. Lou Gehrig's disease. She received the news like the brave forgiving lady that she was. We never openly discussed the ultimate together, but the unpleasant was always in conscious during the quiet and dark hours that one spends alone.

Aliene struggled at first with minor difficulties — stumbling, numbness, etc. Then, as the months passed, it became more necessary to help her get through the day. It became our constant vigil to care for her and make her life acceptable. It wasn't fair for such a gentle and loving lady to be forced more and more to give up her dignity and self-esteem. My wife went to her heavenly home March 28th, 1996 in a gentle and peaceful way.

I am so grateful that I was able to care for Aliene during the period that fate was depriving one thing at a time from her normal pattern of daily living.

Our 54 years were not all perfect harmony, but our maturing years brought us understanding, true affection, responsibility for each other, disappointment and tears, successes and failures. There were harsh words and there were sweet words, approvals and disapprovals.

I miss her. She is constantly in my thoughts. I miss her opinions and our discussions, questions and answers. A 54-year-old symphony is hard to put on a shelf or tuck away in a box. I wear her wedding ring on my neck chain, that way she is as close as a touch. In my many prayers to God, I thank him that I was privileged and able to care for her. I thank him for wrapping his ever-loving arms around Aliene and ask him to give her a hug for me.

Bud Greener

Courage is like love;
it must have hope to nourish it.

Napoleon Bonaparte

A Kiss for Trudy

My granddaughter, Melissa, came into my den accompanied by her doll Trudy. In truth, Trudy was being hauled around by her hair. The hair of the doll was in such disrepair that there was just enough to allow Melissa to get a firm grip on Trudy.

"Good morning, Melissa. Give Poppa a kiss."

Melissa came over and gave me a dutiful peck on the cheek. Then she held an upside down Trudy next to my face.

"You should kiss Trudy, too. You never kiss Trudy." Melissa's face was screwed up into a minor pout.

"Why do you kiss Trudy?" I asked.

"Because I love her."

"Does Trudy ever kiss you back?"

"No, but I pretend that she does."

"Melissa, when you kiss your folks, or Grammy, or Poppa, do we kiss you back?" I tried to soften my voice as much as possible.

"Yes."

"Isn't it better then to kiss us and get some love in return?"

Melissa thought about that comment for some time and then answered me as directly as she could. She apparently was not sure that she could express her feelings in a way that I could understand.

"You and Grammy kiss each other. Mommy and Daddy kiss each other. You all kiss me and I kiss you.

There is no one to kiss Trudy but me. I know she doesn't kiss me, but she needs love and I'm the only one around to give her any love. Is that wrong Poppa?"

"No, it is not wrong. In fact, what you have said is very wise. From now on I promise to help you love anyone that needs love, and I would really like you to bring Trudy with you for our good night and good morning kisses."

"Thank you, Poppa. Can we sit on your lap?"

"Of course you can." I reached out to Melissa and Trudy and lifted them as carefully as I could to a comfortable position on my lap.

Matt Zimmermann

Dost thou love life?
Then do not squander time, for that's the stuff
life is made of.

Benjamin Franklin

Don't Let Go

May 21, 1996 is a day I will remember and cherish for the rest of my life. My eldest son, Dane'll, graduated from high school. It was a day of celebration shared with family and friends. As the school administrator called his name to receive his diploma, I felt years of weight lifted from my shoulders. As I witnessed my son, I remembered the many challenges that I faced as a single parent raising two sons during this time of negative influences confronting us everyday. I began to reflect on the demanding discussions to keep him motivated and to encourage him to stay focused on education. The many games and practices I attended to see him play football, run track and play baseball. The trips to the drug store to stock up on Ben Gay body ointment and Epsom salt to relieve his pain. The many visits to the doctor for x-rays, check-ups, or repair an injury resulting from a game.

I remembered the teacher conferences about "wasted potential" or speaking to teachers on behalf of my son. I remembered asking my son if he had done his homework. I remembered telling Dane'll to get off the phone before it began to grow on his ears. I clearly remembered how I had to continuously convince him that girls are here to stay and he will meet many more. I remembered the heated discussions over the years. I remembered coming home from work one day to find out he had shaved off his curly hair (of course his brother had to tell me first) and how I got through it.

As the final list of graduates was called, I thought about my other son, Theodis, and wondered if his experiences would be the same or different. After the graduation ceremonies, I looked for Dane'll in the crowds of people to hug him and tell him that I loved him and was very proud of his accomplishment. As I began to search for him, and his bald head, he was looking for me. I saw him moving his lips to ask, "Where is my mama?" We finally reached each other. After showing me his beautiful wide smile, he grabbed me as though it was for dear life and cried. I cried, held him and told him how much I loved him. He held me so tight and said, "Thank you for believing in me."

We held each other for so long. I will never forget the feelings and emotions that ran through me, knowing that all we went through as a parent and child was well worth it. I still keep that moment in my heart and thank God that I have it. To know that my son appreciates me as a mother, friend, and role model was all worth it. Life has shown my sons and me that you can't always let go when you are loved. I am loved!

Janet Watson

ESDrbunny
kin you
breg A CANDY
Fr MOMY

From Stephanie

Love Was on Our Side

I will always remember that day many years ago as my mother stepped up to the podium. My dad, sisters and I were beaming with pride and love. My mother was and is such a caring and wonderful person. She had always been there for us and now we were there for her as she was about to have her moment in the spotlight. The award she was about to receive filled us with such great pride and love that it was almost overwhelming. The electricity that filled the room from the other guests heightened the moment.

As my mother spoke, she talked about her experiences and then ended her speech by telling everyone, "If it wasn't for the love of my three girls, I wouldn't be here talking with you today. I now know how much they love me and I want them to know that I love them all very much." Everyone in the room clapped, while we three girls certainly didn't have a dry eye.

You see, five years prior to that day, our mother had once again had too much to drink and we decided we loved her too much to let this continue without at least trying to make a difference. Our father was out of town, so my two grown sisters and I took matters into our own hands. Much to Mom's dismay, we carried her to the car and took her to the hospital to try an overnight detox and hopefully get her to stay in their rehab program. It was a very emotional experience. We were very uneasy about what we had done. We started to question whether it was the right thing, if Mom would be mad, if Dad would be mad. So many things went through our heads. Mainly, we wondered if we would still be loved the next day.

Now, here we were five years later as our mother received her 5-year sobriety award. Luck and love were on our side. Mom and Dad both still loved us. We took a chance and we had made a difference —not just in her life, but in all of ours. We have a great family. We are a family forever changed and I will always remain,

A loved and loving daughter

God loves the world through us.

Mother Teresa

Reassurance

Back when I was a teenager, I was really depressed. My face had broken out with a bad case of acne and my physique was far from athletic. I thought of myself as skinny and unattractive, and was torturing myself. My mom took me aside, and gave me a good lesson in love and life. She said, "You know I wasn't the prettiest girl you ever saw. Your dad on the other hand was really a catch ... tall, dark and handsome ... every girl's dream guy. He didn't fall in love with me for my looks. He loves me for who I am, and how I treat others. It's tough to realize when you're young, but always remember, it's not what you look like that counts. It's how you treat other people that will bring you friendship, respect, and love."

My mom's advice was not just a motherly gesture. It was a great gift of knowledge and love I'll never forget.

Dick Clark

Editor's note: Dick is an entertainment legend and entrepreneur.

Dear Tooth fairy,
I am sorry to
Say But this is
the last time
you will see
me

Love Susan

Silence

Sometimes silence can be a little frightful. In my religious community, the Jesuits, we have the custom of making a retreat once a year. It is a great opportunity to take a week away from the chores, joys and noise of everyday life and retreat into a quiet place of prayer and reflection, solitude and silence. But the silence can be intimidating. Often during the first few days of retreat, I feel reluctant to engage in the silence and, instead, welcome whatever distraction might come along. At times I even bring the distraction with me.

Once, some years ago, the distraction seemed quite justified. My father had been ill and as I began my annual retreat I kept worrying about him, hoping he would pull through, wondering whether I should call and find out, thinking I should have stayed closer to home instead of making a retreat at that time. To add to my worry, on the first day of the retreat, two of the other people making the retreat mentioned in their prayers at Mass that their fathers had died recently. Throughout the next day my anxiety grew and I finally told the retreat director about my concerns. He listened, made some suggestions for prayer and recommended more quiet time. Just what I didn't need, I thought to myself, more silence!

The retreat center was located in a most beautiful spot near the ocean, with a great range of craggy rocks to the south along the coast and a long, wide stretch of sandy beach to the north. On the third day, after attempting to remain quiet and at prayer, I left my room and walked along the rocks. It was late summer and the day was warm. I sat and became mesmerized by the rather gentle sound of the surf as it kept lapping again and again at the rock ledge just below me. Then a seagull appeared, floating to the same recurring rhythm of the waves, yet not in the water but overhead in the light offshore breeze, wings raised then lowered, up and down, ever so calmly. Within me grew a thought that I could hear repeated with each wave of water and wings, "there is so much more, so much more, don't be anxious, there is so much more." Yes, that's right, I thought, why was I so worried about my father, about illness and death. There is so much more to come.

That evening I could hardly wait to report my new insights and discoveries to the director. He listened and again suggested more prayer and silence for the next day. What a miserable next day it turned out to be. Despite the beauty and the quiet of my surroundings and the very positive message the previous day had given, I was now restless again, unfocused. My worry about my father returned and began to slip into self-concern. I felt alone, unloved. I became frustrated, even angry. This retreat was supposed to be a good experience. What was happening! God certainly didn't seem to care much about me. And nobody else did either. That evening, after listening to my complaints, the director suggested more silence for the following day.

Not much changed during the next few days.

Finally at the end of the sixth day I felt worn out and discouraged. I took a long walk along the beach. It was Saturday and the beach, crowded earlier, now at dusk was empty. And quiet. I sat down. A very light breeze stirred. A piece of paper was caught by the wind and crept along the beach toward me until it landed flat against my side. The paper was folded and I didn't pay much attention to it. I got up to leave and picked up the paper to put it in the trash. I could see that something had been written on the inside of the paper. Curious, I unfolded it and saw large printed letters scrawled in a child's handwriting in different crayon colors that read "I LUV YOU." Stunned for a moment, I shook, then laughter took over and I shouted at myself "how many more messages do you need" and I laughed some more and tears came and I cried and gave thanks to God who is good.

Sometimes the silence comes replete with life. And love. For I am loved. You are loved. My father lived another 10 years and enjoyed good health, dying peacefully at the age of 87.

Thomas J. Savage, S.J.

Surrender

In 1964 I was the Boys Work Director at Whatsoever Center, working with low-income kids and trying to develop the sports program with an absolute-zero budget. I had been begging companies for donations of everything from bats and gloves to uniforms and footballs. We had managed to develop 12 teams of energetic kids!

That year had culminated into a very good athletic year and I thought the kids deserved something special for all of their effort, and something that would help build on their enthusiasm. I began planning an "End of the Year Sports Banquet" for the kids and their parents; and had invited all the company representatives who had so generously supported us. We managed to get the food and all the other banquet items donated except for the most important thing. The kids had no trophies!

I tried and tried, but couldn't get anyone to donate the trophies. I was only making $120.00 per week, with a wife and two kids, and just couldn't afford to purchase the trophies myself. I was at a loss. Then I was struck with one of the most important things that God teaches us ... surrender. As I sat at my dining-room table, I slowly surrendered this worry to The Creator. At that point, I looked at where I was sitting ... at all of that precious wood being wasted as our dining-room table. I went and got my radial-arm saw and cut the table into blocks. I then carved diamond shapes into the blocks (for interest) and engraved the kid's names and award onto metal scraps and glued them to the wood. Whatsoever Center had trophies for its Sports Banquet!

By surrendering this worry and attachment to possession, we were able to see potential. Regardless of my wife's thinking at the time, that table was meaningless to us; but redistributed as trophies, it brought a great deal of joy to those kids. It became a symbol that reinforced the work ethic in each of their lives; but more importantly, it demonstrated the love and acceptance each of us needs to feel to succeed at whatever we attempt.

William C. Akers, Jr.

He who is devoid of the power to forgive
is devoid of the power to love.

Dr. Martin Luther King, Jr.

Taffeta Memories

It was the holiday season in 1948, and my high school steady, Gerald Gorman, had asked me to our Christmas Dance. My mother bought yards and yards of shiny red taffeta to make me the prettiest dress I had ever had. Gerald and I had a wonderful time with our friends in the gymnasium, which was festooned with red and green crepe paper and tiny silver bells.

Everyone liked my red dress so much, I wore it again the following Christmas, and the Christmas after that. It became a holiday tradition. Gerald and I were married in 1954, and I continued to wear the red dress every year at Christmas time. Fortunately, my mother had wisely made the dress with ample proportions, so it continued to fit even when I was pregnant.

For a long time the dress seemed indestructible, but in its 20th holiday season, I got the dress out for Christmas and noticed a hole had been torn in the skirt. If I was ever to wear the dress again, I would need some more shiny red taffeta. By this time the store where Mama originally bought the taffeta was out of business, and my mother had become a helpless invalid. I knew she would be disappointed that I could no longer wear the dress, so I took it to her home to show her the problem.

"I'll not be able to wear this dress anymore, Mama," I said. "There is a large hole which would need matching material to fix it. Of course I could never match this material now. I am so sorry. I enjoyed this dress a lot." Though incapacitated, my mother was still resourceful. She directed me to look into her cedar chest. When I did, I found the scraps of shiny red taffeta Mama had saved 20 years for just such an emergency. The dress got repaired, and I continued wearing it at Christmas time.

In 1977, when the dress was 29 years old, our D.A.R. Chapter had its annual Christmas party. We were supposed to bring something old to the party, so I told my mother I would wear the red taffeta dress. On our way we dropped my teen-aged daughters, Gwen and Vicky, off at their high school, where Gwen was to perform in the pom pon squad at a basketball game. The weather was so warm we were not wearing coats, so I was careful to let no one see me in my old dress, lest Gwen and Vicky be embarrassed at their out-of-style mother.

I cautioned the girls to meet us promptly at 9 p.m. outside the gym, because I would have my mother and not only did not want to leave her alone but also was certainly not dressed to be seen by "mod" viewers. They agreed. Mama and I went on to the D.A.R. party and had a lovely time, especially since my invalid mother rarely got to go to such events. Our party ended earlier than expected, so when we arrived at the high school, the girls were not outside. Finding an unusually good parking place, I decided to risk leaving my mother in the car long enough to find someone to get the girls for me.

The basketball game was so intense I could not get anyone's attention. Feeling excruciatingly conspicuous, I slipped into the gymnasium in my obviously aging red taffeta dress. From her place with her pom pon squad at the far end of the gym, Gwen saw me, but she made no move to leave. In fact, she beckoned me toward her! I finally had to stand right in front of the pom pon squad before she could hear me tell her we had to leave.

After we took mother home, I asked Gwen, "Why in the world didn't you leave the game when you saw me come into that gym? I was embarrassed to death to have to walk the length of that basketball court in front of all those people in this red taffeta dress."

Gwen replied, "I had been telling my friends about your dress that Grandma made for you when you were at our high school. And that you and Daddy came to a party here and that you wore the dress to the party a long time ago....and that you and Daddy are still together and that you still wear the dress at Christmas time. My friends thought that was neat, and they wanted to see the dress, so I waved you down so they could all see you in it. We all thought you looked great!"

My anger disappeared. I thanked God for such children, for such a husband, and for such a mother. I still wear the dress on Christmas Eve. My mother has died and the dress is no longer beautiful, but I can scarcely imagine Christmas without it. For the dress personifies so many happy times that will live forever in my memory and make my spirits bright.

Anita B. Gorman

DEAR DAD, I LOVE YOU MORE THAN A ROCK

HAPPY BIRTHDAY LOVE JOSHUA

Thanks, Moms

I feel this is an opportunity to express my love and thanks to my dear mother. I was adopted at birth, and have always known my mother was, and is, my best friend. She has always been there for me, through thick and thin, and there certainly have been some rocky roads along the way. I have a very hard time expressing my feelings. Words do not come easily and I hold all emotions within.

I would like to say that I never desired to seek my birth parents. It was something I never thought about. However, my sister found out about me from her dying grandmother and finding me became her passion.

About six years ago, she succeeded, and my birth mother and three sisters came for a visit. I found out that I also had two brothers and another sister.

Two years ago, a friend and I traveled to one of the brothers' wedding so that I could meet all of the family. I am very glad that I did, because it reassured me how lucky I was to have been adopted by the ones I consider my parents.

That other family cannot get along with each other and has expressed having endured a lot of abuse and emotional trauma. For this, I am very thankful to my birth mother for having given me up for adoption and having the opportunity to have avoided the sorrow and sadness their lives must have endured.

I definitely believe in the faith of God, and that it

was his desire that I was to fill a void in my adoptive parents' lives, and that I should go on to marry and have a husband, four loving children and four beautiful grandchildren to love and cherish.

For this, I give my thanks to both mothers! The one who gave me up for adoption and the one who so lovingly adopted me and has been my strength, along with God the Father.

Bonita Favre

Editor's Note: As Bonita mentioned in her story, she and her husband, Irvin, have four children —Scott, Brett, Jeff and Brandi. They are the co-authors of the "Favre Family Cookbook."

I think of love as a muscle like the heart. It's powerful. It pumps blood through you and keeps you alive and feeling good.

Amanda Innis

My mom got me a fish

On my birthday, she buys me presents.

Talks me in to stuff.

Helps me pick out clothes.

Excellent at making me breakfeast,

Really good at art.

Love Rachel

The Books of Love

This story starts with a man whose entire career was associated with, or centered on, the word love or the idea of love. At the beginning of his career, Elvis Presley's first movie was entitled, "Love Me Tender," from which a mega hit song came, also by the same name. All through the years that I associated with him, he always ended the show, as our closing theme, with a song from the movie "Blue Hawaii," entitled "Can't Help Falling in Love." So from start to finish, so to speak, Elvis had quite an interesting tie-in with love.

Also, interesting, I think, is our society's preoccupation with love. The word love covers an enormous range of emotional descriptions from loving ice cream, God and country, family and friends, our mates, ourselves —even making love. I know Elvis was very much representative of these thoughts, also.

In light of this, one could say that there's an inherent confusion in the ability of the English word "love" to make good sense. It was only until I read a book entitled, "The Four Loves" by C.S. Lewis —the highly gifted and educated author of Christian Apologetics— that I, for the truly first time, began to understand the real meaning of the word. What an eye opening experience I had and I recommend the book to all. In fact, I know that Elvis spent considerable time, as I do now, reading the greatest love story in mankind's history, the Bible, which I also highly recommend for everyone to read, as well.

In love,
Ron Tutt

Editor's Note: Although he has worked with some of the most talented artists in the music business, Ron is best known as the drummer for Elvis Presley (1969-1977) and Neil Diamond, with whom he has worked for the past 20 years.

Love is what makes a crowd disappear when you're with someone.

Elvis Presley

The Brass Button

It was a cool November day about 70 years ago. A baby boy born six months earlier, was in his crib in a place called the Willows, a home for unwed mothers. He'd spent the first six months of his life trying to find a mom and a dad, but he wasn't having much luck. From time to time people would come and peer, pinch and pat, but so far there had been no takers. Time was running out. He couldn't be a sweet loveable and cuddly little baby forever.

On this particular day, a man and a woman had come to the Willows looking for a baby girl, a sweet beguiling female child who would endure herself to them as only a baby girl could do. "No boys for us," the man told the nurse. Their hearts were set on finding "that special little girl." They wouldn't be looking at boys that day.

The man and woman moved from crib to crib checking out each baby girl with great care and giving barely a glance to the boys who were also available. They wanted their chosen child to be a blonde just like the woman and to have the woman's blue eyes. There were three candidates that fit that requirement to a "T" and the couple moved back and forth between the three to decide. Each time they had to pass by one little boy's crib. He must have sensed the urgency of the situation because he grew more animated and vocal each time they passed.

Finally, the man who was dressed in a suit and wore a vest adorned with brass buttons, stopped at the boy's crib to see what the ruckus was all about. Trying to calm the little tyke, he bent over the crib and gave the boy a loving pat.

That was all it took. In a split second the child grabbed a brass button on the man's vest and held on for dear life. The man looked helplessly at the woman and said, "He won't let go."

The woman smiled and said, "Maybe he's choosing us."

"But he's a boy," the man protested.

"I like little boys," the woman responded.

"But he has brown eyes," the man demurred.

"I know, and right now those eyes tell me that he wants to go with us," said the woman. "I'll tell you what," whispered the woman, "If you can uncurl that little hand from your button and walk away, we'll find a blonde, blue-eyed girl; but personally I'd rather have a brown-eyed boy to raise as my son."

So, I chose and I was chosen. I left the Willows with my parents and was the lifetime beneficiary of their love, with due credit to a little brass button.

Robert F. Bennett

Editor's note: Robert "Bob" has passed away since submitting this story.

Transformation

Did you know the butterfly is cellularly wired for wings? When it enters the cocoon stage, wrapping itself up like a mummy, it actually breaks down and reforms again. It does not take the butterfly form from the original shape, but it actually transforms. It locates the cells for wings, and voila, it leaves the chrysalis and birth takes place. I am not talking scientific-ese here, but let's face it; the meta-morphosis of a butterfly is truly a remarkable concept.

I had a best friend, Eleanor, who loved butterflies. She loved their color, their shape, and their ability to flit from here to there so gracefully. Every day she would select one of her vast array of butterfly pins or earrings, and wear them as her stamp, her insignia. I believe she equated the idea of transformation, their transformation, with hers. In other words, she felt that through her problems in life, she was able to learn and grow. She changed her thinking and changed her life.

One day I stood at my kitchen window and noticed a beautiful butterfly doing its dance of flight. I stood and marveled at the fact that it was here so early in the season. Unbeknownst to me, but a few hours earlier, Eleanor had died.

You would have like her. She always had a smile on her face, a laugh in her heart. She oozed friendship and warmth. It was always good to be with her and in her company. I could call her anytime and she would always be ready to set off on some escapade with me. You would have liked her. She was my friend for years and I felt lost without her.

It took some time to decide where to place her ashes. One day, a group of her friends and I gathered together and came to the decision that Block Island in Rhode Island was the perfect place. Not only did she love it there, but we all did. We set off on the ferry with a picnic lunch. We planned to make this a celebration of life, rather than a mourning of death.

We landed on Block Island and walked to a high cliff overlooking the rocks and ocean below. The cliff itself was decked with trees and shrubs. It was a sort of sheltered place on one side, but open to the world on the other side. The air was just right. A cool breeze touched our face, and the sun nestled down on us, making us comfortable and warm and content.

We sat on the grass and gathered in a circle with some sort of ceremonial plan in mind. There were 10 of us and singly, we each spoke from the heart about some incident and some time in space where we had relished Eleanor's company. As we went around the circle, some of us injected humor. Others talked about her and her transformative ways. And, still others drew on some experience that eventually became a part of them because of Eleanor.

It finally came to my turn, and I talked about the butterfly. No sooner had I entered into the story, a butterfly danced into view. A colorful butterfly, out of season. Our mouths opened. We watched it flit from here to there and then disappear. In awe, we all shed some tears. But in that moment I knew we were loved.

I am not presuming to understand the law of life. I will not talk about the death and possible rebirth of who and what we are. But in that moment I knew that the essence of Eleanor touched each one of us in a personal and unforgettable way.

You can call it coincidence. You can call it what you like, but we were there and we were touched with the kiss of a true friend.

Rev. Charlann Walker

A Love Letter

Bompa,

I want to make sure you understand how much I love you. Since it is so difficult to express, I'm writing this letter. I want you to know how important you are to me and that I will miss you so incredibly much when you are gone.

I have always loved the way you listen and relate to people. You join others without judging and you always seem to understand what the other person is experiencing. I have always felt appreciated by you and I wish that I had realized earlier how really important you are to me. We have not spent enough time together over the years and I regret that deeply. I love that you can give advice without seeming arrogant or judgmental. I love that you have always had time for me. I love that we flew kites and boomerangs together. I love that you felt entitled to show your anger and your opinion without trying to prove that it was the only possible opinion. I love your zest for food and for reading. I love your stories and hearing about your life. There are so many things; I can't remember in my sadness. I respect and love you for all these things!

While I have no choice but to let go of your body, I will not let go of these things. These, for me, are your essence and I will keep them with me always. I will make them a part of me and pass them on to your great-grandchildren. You have made my life so much fuller and happier from your presence and your participation. Your essence will live on through me and our descendants and I will tell them all about you.

I wish life wasn't as it is; that you could stay to meet my children; that you could be here to advise and share your experience with me; that you could eat every Christmas breakfast and dinner with us. I really wish you could; I'm so afraid of losing you.

I guess I have to be satisfied to keep the parts in my heart, the parts that can, the parts that really count, and let your body go. I wish I didn't have to; I'll miss you forever.

Love and thanks,

Dewey

Editor's Note: The previous was a letter from Dewey Gaedcke to his grandfather, J.P. McFarland, shortly before Mr. McFarland passed away. Dewey's father, Gilbert Gaedcke, shared it with us.

A Lovely Evening with Dad

"We don't do enough things together," my dad said while sitting at the kitchen table. "One night, just us two should go out," he exclaimed with enthusiasm. Knowing my dad, I could see that this little outing would probably turn into a major ordeal where everything goes wrong. But I couldn't exactly blame him for trying. After all, he was just trying to reach his, now, somewhat foreign, teenage daughter. And I do have to admit that I'm not really very affectionate towards my dad, or really anyone. I figured that one dull night of stupid jokes and pointless conversations wouldn't hurt me, so, from then on I put on a little facade to make it seem like I was excited about our outing.

The next night as we got into the car, we decided to go ice skating. I liked to skate and he used to play some hockey, so I figured that the evening couldn't be a total loss.

As we glided along the shiny, slick ice, I realized that I was having a great time. We raced, twirled and slipped all over the ice for hours in the freezing cold. It was wonderful!

After we finished skating, feeling half-frozen, we walked down to a little coffee shop where we warmed ourselves by drinking boiling hot cappuccinos. Instead of having boring conversations like I expected, we had a wonderful time. It was then that I said, "We should do this more often." His eyes lit up brighter than the brightest star. I saw that all my dad ever wanted was to love me and get my love back.

Jessica Graham

If you judge people,
you have no time to love them.

Mother Teresa

Love Transcends Duty

There was a quadriplegic stricken with polio after his freshman year in college whose mother provided his constant daily needs for 28 uninterrupted years until her death —and without a single murmur, per the testimony of those closest to her.

Heroic? Yes, but mothers occasionally are called upon to do heroic things, and the good ones, many in number, respond. Duty and love combine to furnish the needed motivation.

But what about the college English teacher whose personal interplay with this quadriplegic was restricted to one course for one semester? What prompted the Jesuit priest, Patrick Cummings, to write his afflicted student every other day for 18 years, some 3,300 letters in all? His last, badly scrawled effort was penned from his cancerous deathbed.

Heroic? Yes, but motivated by LOVE in the grandest sense, conferred on one who has no earthly claim on the donor's affections or from whom no earthly benefit is anticipated. Is this not imitative of God Himself?

John M. Jenks

A Perfect Fit

"I am so scared. I don't know how to make my heart stop fluttering."

"I know, sweetheart, and you don't know how helpless this makes me feel. I wish I could jump into your skin and simply take your place."

"I love you so much. Without you at my side I would never be able to face this operation. I never realized all that you would be for me when I said, 'I do.'"

"You have to go now. God bless you. And remember, I'm going to be sitting right outside this operating room door and I'll be praying for you and the doctor until it's all over. I love you."

Rose was about to undergo a serious operation. Doctors had discovered a cancerous growth on her neck. The doctors were "guardedly optimistic," as they say in the medical profession, about the anticipated results of the surgery. It appeared that the tumor was self-contained and hadn't spread to any other parts of the body. With a little chemotherapy, Rose could look forward to many healthy days in the future.

However, there was another issue that was proving to be difficult. In the process of removing the tumor, the doctor would have to sever nerve tissue that controlled the muscular movements of the mouth. As a result, the right side of her mouth would droop severely, and she would have the appearance of a person who had suffered a stroke. Granted, this wasn't a life and death issue, and positioned next to the question of whether Rose would survive at all, it paled into insignificance. Yet the thought that she would have to live the rest of her life and face the world with a sagging mouth, required a tremendous psychological readjustment.

Fortunately the operation was a success. Two days later, looking in a mirror for the first time, the moment of truth arrived. Rose's husband stood next to her. It was a difficult moment for Rose as she looked at her once nicely shaped mouth, now hanging in a most unattractive way. It was then that her husband took the mirror out of her hand and he placed her hand in his. "I think it looks kinda cute," he said. Then, leaning over her face, he contorted his mouth so that it wrapped around her misshapen mouth, and he kissed her. "See," he said, "it still fits."

Father Jim Savage

Kindness in words creates confidence, kindness in thinking creates profoundness, kindness in feeling creates love.

Lao Tzu

A Second Chance for Defining Love

My parents separated about 20 years ago. It happened when my youngest siblings —a sister, Annie, and a brother, Tommy— were very small. They only remember the very rough and difficult time when my mother and father were together. A time when my father's behavior was unacceptable due to alcohol abuse. I always felt that their poor perception of our dad certainly had some validity, but it was unfortunate that there was not balance for them. Because, I, along with my other five siblings, do share a vivid remembrance of many of the wonderful things that made our family a whole and complete family.

My parents enjoyed being together with the children. They danced together during special holiday seasons to entertain us. They built our house together. Daddy felt it was important for his children to learn as much as possible. He taught us how to listen and respect, other people. He walked us to school and to church, teaching us the value of love of people, property and self.

Since Annie and Tommy had little or no fond memories of my father, they never really connected with him in that father-child relationship. This was especially true of Annie; she kept her distance from him. Her lack of interest or involvement was so apparent that we kind of made a joke of the fact that Annie looked like the reflecting image of my dad's youngest sister. (We teased her and said it was a curse.) Fast forward 15 years, and we are now all adults with families of our own. In 1992, my father suffered a severe stroke, causing him to be paralyzed on the entire left side of his body. Then, he had other additional physical and mental complications.

After months in the hospital, we were told that a decision of what to do with him had to be made. He was being released from hospital care. We were then torn by our love, what we believed was Dad's wish and his medical needs. The decision by democratic vote of his children, willed us to take him back to his home, a very small apartment. All eight of his children and my dear mother rallied together and split up duties, took night shifts and hired a nurse during the day. It was coincidental that Annie was on a two-week leave from work. She reluctantly agreed to stay with Daddy during the day until we were able to identify a permanent nurse. Although no one came out and said so, we were very afraid that he would need more care than we could provide for him at his home, therefore requiring the special care of a nursing home. All we knew at the time was that we loved Daddy, even if he had caused us hurt, shame and disappointment in the past. He was our dear daddy.

Annie had been with him for a week. The progress was slow, depressing and nerve wracking for everyone. We continued to pray in overtime. Then, one day I received a telephone call at my office. The receptionist entered the meeting room and told me, "I have an emergency call and it is about your father." My heartbeat rushed, then sank. When I got to the telephone all I could say was, "is daddy alive?"

Annie was on the other end of the line. Her voice was low and quivering. She said, "Ruby, he is fine; Daddy is fine." I was so relieved. Then I asked, "What is it?"

Annie responded in a voice that I will never forget, "Ruby, Daddy moved his hand for me today. He helped me lift his body, he spoke to me and he smiled." Her voice was full of tears. Then, for the very first time in her life she said, "Ruby, I didn't know, but now I do … I LOVE MY DADDY … I REALLY LOVE MY DADDY!" Those were her own words, expressing her newfound feelings.

I am grateful to God for giving us such a wonderful gift. Annie and Daddy recognized and captured their own chance to the special love of father and daughter. They are now inseparable. Our family is now whole and blessed.

Ruby Bright

Above Fear

Our adopted son found his birth mother several years ago. When they met, and she joyously welcomed him, at once, it became clear that she had searched for him throughout her life. Our son was to be married in the fall of that year. I cannot remember how it came about exactly, but the idea of inviting her and his two half-brothers to the wedding was discussed. I, being his mother, felt threatened.

I needed help with this, so I asked a friend who was deeply religious. She said, "How lucky for you that more people have come into your life to give you another opportunity to be loving." I really did not comprehend what this meant. I only knew that I must reach above my fear and insecurity to welcome this woman to that celebration of love. My husband agreed. We thought about the years of joy that we had cherished with this child since his birth and the sense of loss that this woman had experienced. The gift to us that evening was knowing that we were able to rise above fear, to be able to put the love for our son and the woman who bore him, above it.

Barbara Littman

An Unexpected Celebration

I will always remember a wonderful surprise I received when I was 9 years old. I was lying down on the living room carpet, listening to the radio and reading the "funny papers," when someone knocked on our side door. "Will you please see who it is?" asked Mama. "I'm too busy right now."

Reluctantly, I left the funnies, went down the short stairway, and opened the door. There stood a half-dozen or more of my neighborhood friends —my "kick the can," "red light," and card-playing friends— both boys and girls.

"SURPRISE!" they shouted. Mama had invited them for supper.

I was dumb-founded. It wasn't anywhere near my birthday, and there was no cause I could think of for a special celebration. I was thrilled to see them of course, and we all ate and laughed and had a wonderful time together.

Later, I asked Mama, "Why did you do it?"

She smiled and hugged me. "Just because," she said.

Mama didn't exactly say, "Because I love you," but I knew what she meant.

Joan King Holtzman

Birthday Surprise

I love to surprise people. Seeing the amazed expression on their surprised faces is truly a thrill. I have organized surprises ranging from my husband's 21st, 40th and 60th birthdays, and my daughter's 16th birthday, to honor awards events for community leaders. None of them ever detected that a surprise was in store.

Shortly after my 60th birthday, I was pleasantly surprised by a call from my daughter who lives 200 miles away. It was Spring Break and my grandchildren were bored, so they decided to drive in for a visit. We agreed to go to a local favorite restaurant for dinner that evening. As we pulled up to the restaurant, my 6-year-old grandson noticed a huge limousine in front. I asked the driver if my grandson could see the interior of such a luxurious vehicle. The driver graciously opened the door.

Imagine MY surprise when my daughter from Texas and her son, another daughter, and 10 of my very best friends, were all there raising a champagne toast to me. Never had anyone been able to pull a surprise like this on me. At that moment I felt so totally overwhelmed as I realized that this was a reflection of their love and friendship for me. How lucky I am, to be so loved!

The driver offered me a glass of champagne and we drove off, touring the city and spending my special surprise evening at a new restaurant that had just opened. What a wonderful surprise!

Joan Shields

DerGAGa
IJove ♥

An Unexpected
Gift of Love

As a consultant on inheritance issues, I often meet with families to guide and facilitate their considerations of various matters having to do with their wealth, the inheritance process, and their relationships with one another.

Some years ago I was employed to facilitate such a meeting with an extended family group in a southeastern city. The family members who organized this meeting warned me a number of times that "Bill," one of the members of the senior generation, was unalterably, almost violently, opposed to my being there and to what he anticipated would happen in and to the family as a result of my participation. He categorized the process as "group therapy," making it clear that this could only do harm to the individuals involved and to the family as a whole. He went on to say that, if the meeting sponsors did insist on going ahead as planned, he would take no part in the portions of the meeting I would be facilitating.

With some misgivings on their part, and considerable misgivings on mine, the family went ahead as planned. When we first met, "Bill" was just barely civil to me and was clearly unimpressed by my attempts at charming him. When the meeting started, he moved his chair some 10 feet outside of the circle, refused to answer questions, and made it painfully clear that he was there only as a skeptical and critical observer.

As the meetings proceeded, it became evident that none of the negative results that he had anticipated were happening. People began talking to each other in ways they hadn't before, old wounds and resentments were shared and cleared up, and, over the two days, a remarkable feeling of caring and affection was palpably growing in the room. People who had barely spoken to each other for some time began to express their care for one another, often tearfully. While we worked on issues having to do with wealth and its transfer, love and forgiveness became more and more evident among the family members.

"Bill" soon moved in to become a vital part of the group. While it was clearly difficult for him to express emotions, particularly positive ones, he was increasingly able to let people know, in his way, that he cared about them and wanted to be helpful in their lives. They, of course, responded appropriately, and a number of the younger members got past their fear and suspicion of this man and made it clear that they could put past wounds behind them. They were just delighted that he was becoming so much a participant and caring member of the family.

At the end of the weekend, "Bill" conveyed to me his appreciation for the contribution I had made and his hope that our relationship could continue. It was difficult for me at that point to keep my voice steady and to hold back any evidence of tears, which I felt I had to do to avoid embarrassing him painfully.

Thinking about him and our experience together can still elicit a sense of joyful tearfulness for me.

John L. Levy

Life is the first gift, love is the second,
and understanding the third.

Piercy

Typically Adele

Adele has always considered birthdays to be great events and "surprises" supreme! It should be no surprise, then, that she has planned spectacular surprise parties for me on special birthdays.

On my 50th birthday, she reserved a large suite at a wonderful hotel. Because of my fondness for the Japanese (I served in Japan for 16 months in the early 1950s), and for Japanese food, she orchestrated a surprise party complete with sushi, sashimi, sukiyaki, shabu shabu, and other marvelous Japanese dishes. The food was served by colorfully-costumed waitresses, and devoured in traditional Japanese style, by most, but not all of the guests —our closest friends. One friend found it a little difficult to use the floor as a chair for the duration, while another complained that "It wasn't until the seventh course that we got anything to eat that was cooked!" In spite of those and other good-natured comments, it was wonderful!

On my 60th, things became much more elaborate. Many out of town guests were invited to surprise me, each of whom had special meaning to me. Many were friends from long ago, including a high school buddy whom I had not seen for years. That friend, Jim Wade, had grown a beard in the intervening years, and that night had come dressed as a hotel waiter, complete in official uniform and name badge, "James." When I arrived, he walked up to me and offered my favorite drink. Although surprised, excited, and distracted by the crowd, I still knew the drink did not taste quite right, and put it back on the tray. "James" insisted it was the right beverage, and brought it back on the tray. After three or four of these exchanges, he feigned exasperation, and drank it down! Thinking this was not proper behavior for a waiter, I looked at him more closely, and only then recognized my high school friend. We had a great hug, and onlookers said they detected extra moisture on both our faces. What a blast, a real surprise, and typically Adele.

Don Hall

Editor's Note: Don Hall, current chairman of the board for Hallmark Cards, was the chief executive officer of the company from 1966 until 1986. His father, Joyce C. Hall, founded Hallmark in 1910. The next story is by Don's wife, Adele.

If you wished to be loved, love.

Seneca

Anniversary Memories

Our wedding anniversaries have always been extremely special to us. Even though we have known each other for 66 years, and have been married for 46, that special date of November 28 has never lost its sense of importance and deep meaning to us.

Although our anniversary falls during the busy Thanksgiving holiday time, we always take time to celebrate in a very unique and memorable way.

In the early years, just going out to dinner was a great celebration, momentarily escaping the responsibilities of children and business. On our fifth anniversary, we visited friends in Minnesota, as they had us on their fifth anniversary ... the happy result of a college pact made between two Dartmouth buddies a few years back.

But the standard celebration was going out to dinner in a quiet spot to reminisce, to give thanks, and to re-commit to all those things which make a marriage good and strong and lasting.

When the Crown Center Hotel, now the Westin, opened in Kansas City in 1971, our anniversary became even more special! Donald had arranged a surprise dinner in the traditional quiet way, except this time it was in a small suite at the hotel! He had pre-planned a small arrangement of flowers for the candlelit dining table, set for a wonderful dinner by the fire, music, and a gift complete with many silly and sentimental cards to be opened later. As the evening unfolded, I discovered more surprises, including my overnight case that he had carefully packed! It was truly an occasion to remind me of how much I am loved.

Layers of memories have been built upon that special surprise of 29 years ago as each anniversary has been celebrated in similar fashion (although I now do the packing myself!). Still, I always act terribly surprised, because I know Donald loves to surprise me! And I love surprises!

Many memories and sentimental gifts have marked this special date, which all began when a 6-year-old boy and a 3-year-old girl met quite by chance. I often wonder how the next anniversary will be celebrated, but I will never wonder whether or not I am loved.

Adele Hall

If you would be loved, love and be lovable.

Benjamin Franklin

Dear Mom and Dad

I want to thank you for
all the special things you have given
me. The first thing is when I an
sick you are there. The second
thing is my go cart racing and
all the times I have wrecked, you
told me to get back out there.
The third thing I would like to
thank you for is when I had
stitches in my lip you were
there holding my hand

With love
Larry xoxxo

What is Love?

"A kiss from Mom."
— Zach, 7-years-old

"When my Mom and Dad hug me."
— Tatum, 6-years-old

"When people tell you a bunch of times every day"
— Bailey, 6-years-old

"When Grandma and Grandpa make sure you don't get hurt."
— Kaylee, 7-years-old

"When there is a little trouble and someone sends you a love note."
— Nathan, 6-years-old

"When Grandma sends me a card and puts $2.00 in it."
— Dylan, 6-years-old

"The feeling when my baby sister was born."
— Destany, 7-years-old

"When someone hugs you and helps you with your homework."
— Sha, 7-years-old

"When someone from far away sends you a package."
— Keiffer, 7-years-old

"When Mom reads a book and listens to you."
— Victoria, 6-years-old

"When my sister wants to stick around me all the time."
— Riley, 6-years-old

"When my Mom tries to do fun things for me."
— John Andrew, 6-years-old

To Dad Form Dave I Love My dad

I AM LOVED

A Mother's Legacy

I learned at an early age through my mother, that I am loved. She served as my role model and her example taught me to recognize love, as well as give it to, and receive it from, all kinds of people.

My mother devoted her life to helping others, specifically as the founder of a national Braille volunteer organization. For 30 years, she organized workers all over the country to transcribe school textbooks into Braille for blind children to use so they could learn in the same classrooms as sighted children. I traveled with her often to meet with the many devoted and loving volunteers, and to take books to the blind adult volunteers who spent hours proofreading the books. I also met blind children who were happy to receive these books so they could use them in their classes. I learned at an early age that love came from all kinds of people. I learned that they were just like us, they just couldn't see with their eyes. They could see very clearly with their hearts and their other senses. I learned at an early age that they genuinely loved me. The blind people that I knew and grew to love were positive, giving and fun people. My mother taught me through her actions that what matters most, is not what the eyes can see but what the heart can see. I consider this a gift that my mother gave to me which through her example, provided me the foundation for understanding that people with disabilities are just as capable as loving and feeling and being as valid and respected as people without disabilities. She taught me that what really is most important is inside the soul of each person. I have come to realize how she showed me I was loved, which was important for me to show others they are loved by me and what great joy that brings.

Now, fast-forward to my adult life. My mother has passed away. I was looking for a wife, a partner with which to spend the rest of my life. I had spoken to many prospects. That is, women that my friends recommended. While talking with these women on the phone, I came upon one very special woman who was as busy as I was. Our schedules did not permit us to get together in person for some time. Yet, we spoke on the phone daily and got to know each other intimately over the next few weeks through lengthy and frequent telephone conversations in the evenings. I found myself loving this woman without ever having seen her. It dawned on me that I had, in fact, "fallen in love" with Julie through our conversations over the phone, based upon criteria seen by my heart. I understood what it must be like for a blind person to see things without the use of their eyesight. I was able to focus on her inner beauty, which is what is most important in a person. Somehow, it didn't matter as much to me what she looked like. I guess these lessons of love my mother showed me over all those years prepared me for that moment. Oh, by the way, Julie and I married, and had a son who was named after my mother.

Now, fast-forward even more and our son, Daniel, is

now 5 years old. We have told him consistently about how to appreciate the things that are important in life. For instance, when we watch a fireworks display, we close our eyes and image what it would be like to be blind. When we open our eyes we can appreciate the sight that we have. Recently at Daniel's school, his teacher asked the children in her class to draw a picture of what they were thankful for. His teacher gave us his picture during a parent-teacher conference. He was thankful for his eyes. The love that came from his grandmother, through his father, is now a part of him. My wish is that he will always know that he is loved. This important foundation will help him be prepared to deal with his life and priorities in the proper perspective, and pass this love on to his loved ones, so that they too will know that they are loved.

Brian Hakan

Knowledge is gained by learning;
trust by doubt; skill by practice;
and love by love.
Thomas Szasz

Aunt Della

I learned at an early age that love is so incredibly powerful. When I was 12 years old, my mother and father got a divorce, so I moved to New York City to live with my aunt Della. That was a life-changing experience. My mother was a very strict disciplinarian. I knew she loved me, but she didn't express love in the conventional way.

Aunt Della was just the opposite of my mother. Aunt Della was bubbly, laughed and had fun all the time. And she made chocolate chip cookies. Living with her was such a joy. My whole world changed. She started me on a love affair with chocolate chip cookies at the age of 12, that still goes on to this day.

I can remember sharing a small, one-bedroom apartment with Aunt Della, her husband, and their son, Joe, with whom I shared a bed in the living room. She'd make cookies in this small kitchen that they had, and I'd sit there, anxiously, eagerly, waiting for her to finish making those cookies. (Not only could I not wait for the cookies to finish baking, but while we were waiting, I'd get to lick the spoon and the bowl!) Then the cookies would come out of the oven ... mmmm, mmmm. I can't express in words how simply fantastic those cookies tasted. Even today as I tell people the story, I can still taste, smell and picture that experience.

I know the love that Aunt Della put into those cookies is still with me. She passed away before I started Famous Amos, but I always felt that she was my guardian angel. I felt she was always protecting me. She gave me a very deep appreciation, a deep love, of chocolate chip cookies. I think the same love that was in Aunt Della's chocolate chip cookies, has been transferred to everything that I do. Love, after all, is transferable.

Wally "Famous" Amos

Editor's Note: Besides chocolate chip cookies and muffins, Wally Amos has a love for children and education. He currently is involved in developing "READ ALOUD with Wally Amos," a children's reading program in partnership with public television. Through the series, Wally shares, among other things, the adventures of his two characters, named — appropriately enough — Chip and Cookie.

Card Partners

"There's a patient down the hall looking for somebody to play cards with," was the message I heard. I was also a patient in St. Francis Hospital in Evanston, Illinois in 1962, recuperating from an emergency appendectomy. A couple days before, I had been operated on at midnight, after lying on a bus most of the day with a terrible pain in my side during our nursing school's annual picnic.

It was Friday night, my friends had gone home for the weekend, I was 19 years old, and the opportunity to play cards at that moment sounded pretty good. I hobbled down the hall in my pink robe and slippers, looking like somebody does after having major surgery … no makeup, unwashed hair and stooped over.

As I entered the room of the patient wanting to play cards, I saw this tall, lanky, dark-haired young man with this nose bandaged. When he told me his name was Steve Israelite, I was especially intrigued, because I was in the middle of reading "Exodus" in the Bible, and had never known anyone who was Jewish. I had gone to Catholic schools all my life in Joliet, Ill., which was pretty much a Catholic town.

Steve and I never did play cards that evening. Once we started talking, we didn't stop. He was the most intriguing person I had ever met, nothing like any of the guys I had dated. He knew so much about so many things. Plus, his quick wit kept me amused. He was interested in poetry, religion, art, music and philosophy. We talked until the head nurse intervened saying that visiting hours were over and I really needed to return to my room. That night, I made an entry in my diary, about marrying him.

The next day, Steve came to my room and helped me fill out my breakfast menu. I remember laughing so hard that I thought I would burst my stitches. That afternoon, he was discharged, but called that evening and came to see me the next day. He brought me a book about the Bahai religion, which fascinated both of us (Evanston has one of the world's most beautiful Bahai Temples). We talked about how he was going to fix me up with his Catholic friend, Frank Nicolella. We would double with Steve and his longtime girlfriend, Francis.

He was going to come visit me again the following day, when I was unexpectedly discharged early because my bed was needed for another patient. I was sent home to Joliet for a month before I could return to nursing school. I dropped a note to Steve telling him that if he and his girlfriend were near Joliet, to come visit and that I would be returning to school a month later.

While I was home, I already began talking with my priest about a potential "mixed marriage." On the night that I returned to school four weeks later, I was in the shower when my roommate came running in to tell me that Steve was on the phone. I, of course, didn't believe her because we were always playing tricks on each other to get into the coveted shower stalls that were shared by 40-plus nursing students.

When she finally convinced me, I ran to the one payphone in the long hall, wrapped in a towel. Sure enough, after a month with no communication, I heard Steve's voice on the other end of the phone. As the night watchman exited the elevator, I had to quickly end the conversation. We made quick plans to go to Grant Park in Chicago for a symphony concert the following evening. It was my first symphony concert.

Listening to that concert on the grass next to Lake Michigan cinched what I had already suspected the night I first met Steve. I was in love. I remember writing an epic poem about my feelings that evening that began with: "All of a sudden you know it. You know what it means to be in love, after wondering if it will ever happen to you."

Two years later, that same priest who I talked with during my recuperation, married us. Shortly afterwards, we left for two years service in the Peace Corps in Brazil.

After 35 years of marriage and two sons, I converted to Judaism and we were married again; this time in a Jewish ceremony. We are one of the few couples who now celebrate two wedding anniversaries.

We never did play cards. We just fell in love.

Joan Israelite

Chain of Gratitude

As Thanksgiving Day approached nearly 20 years ago, my wife, three young children and I attended Sunday morning mass at the active Jesuit parish. On that Sunday, a spectacled old Jesuit from the college across the street was preaching and officiating at the service.

During his homily he challenged us to think of someone in our past who had helped us in some way, large or small. He said to think about a person we seldom think of and reflect on an act of kindness, generosity, or a challenge that ultimately affected our lives.

Within moments I was thinking of my eighth-grade teacher, Sister Claire Louise. In this flashback, I was once again the class president and conducting our weekly class meeting. Since I had not prepared anything, I struggled to think of something to say, as my subjects became restless. Sister interrupted the meeting saying, "It is obvious that you are not prepared and nothing is getting accomplished. This meeting is over."

Of course, I was embarrassed at the time, but, probably, I was more relieved. Could this be my opportunity to get out of this job and never have to get up in front of a group again? I approached Sister at lunch, apologized and suggested, "I think it would be a good idea to elect a new president because I'm not a leader." Sister stared right through me with her deep blue eyes and replied, "You are, too. You just aren't accepting your responsibilities. You are lazy and you are president! Now get yourself prepared for next week's meeting."

You bet I did! Since this encounter with "tough love," I frequently find myself in front of groups. As a college professor, you better believe that I am prepared when I walk into the classroom —even my ad-libs are rehearsed. Sister Claire could have taken the easy way out and let me slip by, but she insisted that all her students set high standards and strive for them.

"Where is this remarkable lady?" I thought.

I sent a letter to her mother's house in Wichita, Kan., to trace her. I learned that she was alive and well and working as a librarian 2,000 miles away. I struggled as I wrote a thank you note to her, but I had to tell her what a wonderful person she is and what a tremendous influence she had on my life through this seemingly insignificant incident. I mailed this "thank you note" while wondering if she would even remember me, much less this occurrence.

To my surprise, I received a letter back within a week. Sister not only remembered me and the incident, but also reminded me of other events that I had long forgotten. But, most of all, she was thrilled that I still remembered her!

Every member of our family sent a "thank you" note that year to a special person. Composing each letter was exciting. We had fun reminiscing —even our 5 year old— and each person we wrote to, wrote us back! They were pleasantly surprised by the notes and, in their own way, said that our thoughtfulness "made their day." Their responses, in turn, made ours!

I have given a couple of college commencement addresses since that homily and the "thank you note" became an integral part of each talk. That's right, when you ask a college professor to speak, you get an assignment —the most important assignment I give.

Our family is grown and scattered now. However, we all have a powerful tool that this marvelous Jesuit gave us in his sermon years ago —and we need not wait until Thanksgiving to use it. Though Father Bro is no longer with us, I must tell him, "Thanks for teaching us a simple way to share our love."

Dick Shaw

Love looks through a telescope;
envy, through a microscope

Josh Billings

I'm special because __I am__
__loved.__

Michelle

Creating A Memory

My fondest memories of early childhood
are of my father reading the fairy tale,
"Rapunzel," to me. The deep timbre of
his voice still resonates in my mind today as he would
begin, "Once upon a time..." Although my parents did
not graduate from high school and there were few
traditions in my family, reading was always an
important event. Many of the lessons I value in life
had their beginnings in the stories and fables of my
childhood.

Years later, my daughter, Senara Rose, was born
two months early and weighed only 4-pounds, 6-
ounces when we brought her home. She suffered from
an infected birthmark on her thigh and needed to be
held and comforted frequently. Reading seemed to
soothe her, and thus our family tradition was
re-established. Senara's first poem, "Hush Little Baby,"
and first book, "Good Night Moon," are still among
her favorites.

Story times have become a ritual with my
daughter. Life has been hard at times. Senara's father
and I are no longer together, and it's not always easy
for me to be the reassuring parent she needs. But no
matter how difficult the day has been, at night we
cuddle under the quilt and read. It's during this
precious hour that I hope to create a small memory of
love.

As I learned life lessons from my father reading to

me, I've also learned them by reading to my daughter. There is one book that I find especially poignant, which has provided me with valuable insight, "I'll Love You Forever," by Robert Munsch. It is the story of a mother holding her newborn son, rocking and singing, "I'll love you forever. " The boy grows to be a man, and when his mother is very old and very sick, he holds her and sings that he will "love her forever." The first time I read this book to Senara, I cried. She put her arms around me and said, "Don't worry, mommy. I'll love you forever and like you always." Then I realized that, no matter what happens in my life, and what changes occur, there is one constant. Senara is my daughter, and I'm her mother, and our love for each other will always endure.

So each night, I fluff the pillows, pull the quilt tightly around Senara, open a book, and begin reading, "Once upon a time ..."

Rosalie Sanara Petrouske

I am praying for you.

Everything's Great

It had been one of those very tough weeks at the Kidwell household. My husband, Bob, was out of town on a business trip in New York. I was trying to juggle the usual demanding work schedule, MBA school evening classes, while making sure our three dogs and one cat hadn't forgotten how precious they are to us. Our two teenagers were very focused on their individual school scenes. Our daughter, Becky, was a busy senior in high school. Our son, Robbie, was in his junior year at college.

Both Robbie and Becky had the typical teenage mindset: I'm mature, I'm capable, I'm independent, but I may need a little money for this weekend, please. So, when there was a message left on our home recorder from Robbie, I wasn't concerned. His father, meanwhile, was involved in numerous meetings while in New York and Robbie had left two messages there before his father had an opportunity to call him back. Not receiving an answer when we each called Robbie, Bob and I talked long-distance to see if everything was all right.

The next day, Bob received another urgent message to call Robbie at school. Naturally, one's mind begins to think of some pretty horrible things at this point. Finally, after numerous phone calls, Robbie and his father connected live. Robbie's voice was very calm. He chatted about school, work, and what was going on that weekend, as though providing a short news story.

Still concerned, Bob spoke up, "Is everything OK, Robbie? I've been trying to call you for two days since you left me that urgent message. Is something wrong at school? Are you sick?"

Robbie was a little silent at first and then just said, "Oh, everything's great. I just wanted to tell you how much I missed you and loved you, Dad."

Renee Kidwell

Love people. Use things. Not vice versa.

Kelly Rothaus

Fifty Years of Life and Love

Half a century . . . A very special celebration was in order. A youthful-looking mother of two and a tremendously devoted wife for 30 years, Mary Lea Shore deserved a real birthday surprise for her 50th birthday.

Having secretly designed a special invitation, I mailed 90 of them to our closest friends and relatives. Then, lots of follow-up phone calls were made from the office.

Buying up most of the house, I purchased theater tickets at a local dinner playhouse. The play, called "Under Papa's Picture," was a comedy staring Elinor Donahue. The story was about a widow who just turned 50, and tells her businessman son, John, that she is going to be a mother again, even though she has yet to remarry.

On Mary Lea's birthday, I arrived at home and announced that we had tickets for us and our son and his wife, to attend that night's performance to celebrate. Everyone showed enthusiasm for the idea, so together we proceeded to the theater.

Meanwhile, at the theater, having been encouraged to arrive early, the guests were in place. Almost every table was filled with our friends. Quietly anticipating our arrival, everyone was ready with cards and gifts eager to extend their birthday greetings and love. When Mary Lea realized that everyone had come in honor of her birthday, overwhelmed, she buried her face in my neck to hide her tears of joy. Without any doubt, Mary Lea understood my love for her, and the tremendous sacrifice of my heart. She has said that she felt deeply treasured. Hand-in-hand, and spilling over with emotion, we visited every table and greeted Mary Lea's guests before the performance.

I am so blessed and fortunate to have Mary Lea for my wife. The cost of the tickets and the work that went into the surprise party was all worth it. Celebrating this special occasion with our friends is a wonderful blessing. Throughout the evening, I was beaming with joy; not because I pulled off a great surprise party, but because I truly adore Mary Lea and was honored to make such a loving tribute to the most important person in my life.

After the last curtain call, Elinor Donahue came out on stage and wished Mary Lea a happy birthday. "I have never experienced a performance where I could feel the love of an entire audience like I felt tonight. Thank you, Mary Lea and John, for making this such a special evening."

John H. Shore

I KNOW MY PAPA LOVES Me even Though He Died I Miss Him But His Spirit is Still Alive by Daniel

Editor's Note: Four-year-old Daniel Hakan had been given a helium-filled balloon by his father, Brian. As they were walking, they started talking about Daniel's grandpa who was no longer living. All of a sudden, Daniel spontaneously released his balloon and let it fly away. When Brian asked his son why he did that, Daniel replied, "I want to give this balloon to Papa up in heaven." This drawing by Daniel represents that exchange, with Daniel in the center, Brian at right, and the balloon on the left.

Friends, Indeed

After almost 27 years, my marriage ended in divorce in 1995. The final moment of decision came as my wife and I sat in our car in front of our church one Sunday morning.

I remember turning to her and saying, "I don't know whether to go home with you and wrestle this thing to the end, or stay here at church with the people who have become my family." For that's how I had come to understand my church.

Well, we did go home and we made the hard decisions we had to make.

But that week I wrote a note explaining what was happening to old friends, Charlie and Diana, who used to be members of my church. They now live some four hours away.

That next Saturday night, Charlie worked until 2 a.m. He then went home to Diana, got less than four hours of sleep and, without telling me they were coming, drove several hours that Sunday morning just to go to church with me. They came to be with me, to reach out to me in my pain and loss.

That's love. That's family. That's what a family does for you. That's who we are called to be for one another. That day Charlie and Diana were, as part of my family of faith, channels of God's grace and love.

As Esther DeWaal writes in her lovely little book on the Rule of St. Benedict, "Living with Contradiction," "The promise is not that we shall not be afraid. It is that we need not fear fear." How profoundly true that is for people who have found themselves surrounded by a loving family of faith, surrounded by people like Charlie and Diana.

Bill Tammeus

Love yourself first and everything else falls into line.
You really have to love yourself to get anything done in this world.

Lucille Ball

Gammy's Gift

A child's love is invariably given with a trusting heart and wide-eyed enthusiasm. Their love is so pure, so honest, so simple, so uncluttered. I know!

One night, on a "school night" about 9:00, my telephone rang. An 8-year-old grandson responded to my "hello" with, "I'm upstairs gettin' ready for bed and I was just thinkin' about you. I decided to call and tell you, good night, Gammy, and I love you lots!"

What a gift to a Gammy! The best gift of all —one that can't be bought or sold— just shared!

Mrs. W. Coleman Branton

FoR

Are Good

DaDDY

Gold Endures

Did you ever stop and think of your friendships as either golden friends or silver friends? You are a fortunate person to be able to count on one hand the number of truly golden friendships that you have. The golden ones know all there is to know about you and still, they love you. With the years of shared experiences with the golden friendships, you just know you are loved and you love in return. The deep friendships remain through life no matter what changes life brings.

We surround ourselves with our silver friendships most of the time. They are fun and make us feel good, but for the most part, are for the moment and on the surface. There's nothing wrong with having scores of silver friends. Along the way, one of them just may turn into one of gold.

I recently lost a golden friend to cancer and it couldn't have hurt me more deeply if he had been my blood relative. I was there when he died and was so glad he knew I was there along with his family who are almost as close as my own family. His last words to me said it all. "Old friend, we've been through a lot, haven't we?"

As I grow older, it continues to amaze me that the human capacity for love is so boundless. Even after we have deep love for a mate, protective love for our children, respectful and caring love for our parents,

what's left over for those golden and silver friends
stretches into infinity.

Dot Hagman

*Love is the beginning of the journey, its end,
and the journey itself.*

Deepak Chopra

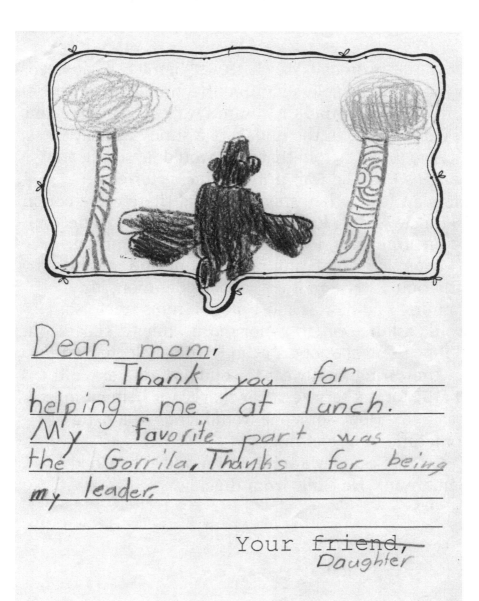

Dear mom,
    Thank you for helping me at lunch. My favorite part was the Gorrila, Thanks for being my leader,

                    Your friend,
                    Daughter

The Good Samaritan

Sunday, March 19, 1995, my car had been hopelessly mired in a muddy field west of Mound City, Kan. I walked to a store and asked for help. In the middle of a sunny Sunday afternoon, I was told that help would be scarce and perhaps I should wait until business started on Monday. It was then suggested that there was a couple in Bigelow, Kan. known for helping people in need, "even strangers." I was told to call Bud Panning.

I contacted Mr. Panning by phone and told him my situation. After a moment of consideration, Mr. Panning said he was short of fuel in his tractor but would ask his wife to go for more while he started out. "I'll be there as soon as I can." What welcome words.

After bringing my car to solid ground I asked the charge for his services. "No charge for helping folks," I was told. "Hope someone would lend me a hand sometime," Mr. Panning said.

On that Sunday afternoon I found "The Good Samaritan." He came from Bigelow.

Tod Haren

Grandpa's Girl

There is nothing like being a parent. That is for obvious reasons. You could say that twice I've been able to be a parent because I have a son and a daughter. But then I stop and think that really the second time around might be the best … that's when you have a grandchild. My granddaughter arrived on this earth in 1989.

Erica and I have always had this relationship. I am her Papa —although I'm not a Hemingway by any stretch of the imagination. One day, when she was 3 years old, my daughter brought Erica to my house so I could keep her for a couple of hours before taking her to a playground session with some of her friends. On the way to the playground, she decided she wanted a taco. We went to a nearby taco spot, which is one that she adored very much.

At the time, I had a big sedan; not a great luxury car, but a big sedan, nonetheless, with heavy doors. We had parked at a little bit of a leaning angle towards the driver's side. I got out of the car saying, "Erica, I'll come around to let you out and we will go get your taco." As I arrived on the opposite side of the car, her door popped open and out she jumped, all 3-feet of her.

She looked me in the eye and said, "You know what, Papa? For such a little girl I'm pretty darn strong, aren't I?" I was so enamored with her at that moment that I would have bought that little girl 10 dozen tacos if she wanted them.

We looked at each other and fell in love again. I've been in love with this one since 1989 and I hope to live a lot longer so I can be in love with her a lot more.

Jim Phillips

Editor's Note: Since 1968, Jim has been the radio "voice" of the Clemson University Tigers.

That best portion of a good man's life,
His little, nameless, unremembered
acts of kindness and of love.

William Wordsworth

Gus's Granddaughter

I distinctly remember having him around at birthday parties and sitting on his lap at Thanksgiving at my aunt's house. I always loved him. I knew he always loved me. That was understood, but at the time we never really talked. He had three other grandchildren, and two of them were older. He had more in common with them. He wasn't like my other set of grandparents. I didn't call him to share accomplishments or just talk. I always enjoyed seeing him, but we lacked a special bond. He had his life and I had mine. He died when I was 8 years old. I felt horrible. I didn't even think I would feel as bad as I did. I was heartbroken for a while.

Time healed the wounds. Four years later, I found myself at his sister's (my great-aunt's) funeral. All of their friends were talking and reminiscing as I wandered by. An old man stopped and asked who I was. I told him. He instantly said, "Oh, you're Gus's granddaughter. He was so proud of you. " I smiled at the man and went on. I deeply began to miss my grandfather again. To this day, those words have made such a difference in my life. I know my grandfather loved me enough to talk about me so much that four years later an old man would still remember me. I think of that old man as a messenger from Grandpa.

Joanna Wright

Hatch

Our fourth and fifth children were identical twin boys. They were our last ones to go off to college. One of them went to Southern Methodist University in Dallas, and the other one went to the University of Southern California in Los Angeles. The freshman orientation was exactly at the same time, so my wife and I flipped a coin to see who would take which son to which orientation. She took Stewart to SMU and I took Hatch to USC. Hatch had been on the campus only once before then, and he didn't know a single person. We went through the traditional two to three days of orientation with various lectures and standing in lines. Hatch and I had spent a wonderful few days together.

I had an early morning flight back home. Before I left for the airport, I went to Hatch's room. He was in there by himself, seated at his desk facing the window, with his back to me. We talked for a few minutes before it occurred to me that there was a reason he wasn't looking at me. So I walked over to his desk, and when he turned around, tears were pouring down both cheeks. That melted my heart. That's all I needed to know of what our relationship was. Even today, nearly 20 years later, I get all choked up thinking about it. I'll never forget that.

Harry McCray

I Am Loved

Since the age of 12 I have been in love with advertising. I have sketched and re-sketched many ads in my day. At 33 years of age in 1967, I found another true love, who emotionally and intellectually was the ideal mate for me.

Shirley Bush accepted my marriage proposal and I wanted to tell the world. To know that she said "yes," knowing that I was loved, made me euphoric!

Perhaps the combination of waiting 33 years and being so powerfully affected emotionally, created the somewhat obnoxious phenomenon of a person who wore the fact that they were in love on their sleeve. I was probably not very pleasant to be around then.

Based on the combination of my two true loves of advertising and Shirley, I was sketching an ad at home one night. It said, "Give her a button or a diamond ($50 to $5,000), but tell her she's loved."

Upon looking at the ad with the crude illustration that showed the I Am Loved® button, I promptly decided that it was far too embarrassing to show the others, so I threw it in the wastebasket. Fortunately for some reason, I pulled it out and snuck it into the office the next day showing it to Claude Burke, a highly talented artist who had been with our family jewelry company approximately 38 years. When I showed the idea to him, he said, "I like it."

After showing the idea to my brother and father, as well as several other Helzberg Diamonds and advertising people, the button and campaign were launched. Little did we expect, the demand for buttons exploded. Our initial order of 50,000 buttons was gone almost immediately. We had to create many, many emergency orders, so as not to disappoint our friends and customers.

Since that day, more than 35 million buttons —in nine languages— have been distributed worldwide. It's been a wonderful trip and the stories of its use all over the world, in all kinds of situations, have been very rewarding for all of us who have been associated with the button. I have traveled to far reaches and have run into people wearing the button, which has been quite a thrill, too.

Perhaps the 33-year popularity of the button is indicative of the feeling so deep within each of us that our prime desire is to be loved!

Fortunately after 33 years, I have the same feeling as the three words disclose when I think about my relationship with my wondrous Shirley May Bush.

Barnett Helzberg, Jr.

In the Trenches

You've probably heard the powerful story coming out of World War I of the deep friendship of two soldiers in the trenches. Two buddies were serving together in the mud and misery of that wretched European stalemate (one version even identifies them as actual brothers). Month after month they lived out their lives in the trenches, in the cold and mud, under fire and under orders.

From time to time one side or the other would rise up out of the trenches, fling their bodies against the opposing line and slink back to lick their wounds, bury their dead, and wait to do it all over again. In the process, friendships were forged in the misery. Two soldiers became particularly close. Day after day, night after night, terror after terror, they talked of life, of families, of hopes, of what they would do when (and if) they returned from this horror.

On one more fruitless charge, "Jim" fell, severely wounded. His friend, "Bill," made it back to the relative safety of the trenches. Meanwhile Jim lay suffering beneath the night flares. Between the trenches. Alone.

The shelling continued. The danger was it its peak. Between the trenches was no place to be. Still, Bill wished to reach his friend, to comfort him, to offer what encouragement only friends can offer. The officer in charge refused to let Bill leave the trench. It was simply too dangerous. As he turned his back, however, Bill went over the top. Ignoring the smell of cordite in the air, the concussion of incoming rounds, and the pounding in his chest, Bill made it to Jim.

Sometime later he managed to get Jim back to the safety of the trenches. Too late. His friend was gone. The somewhat self-righteous officer, seeing Jim's body, cynically asked Bill if it had been "worth the risk." Bill's response was without hesitation.

"Yes, sir, it was," he said. "My friend's last words made it more than worth it. He looked up at me and said, "I knew you'd come."

Stu Weber

Excerpted from "LOCKING ARMS" © 1995 by Stu Weber.
As seen in "Stories For A Man's Heart" © 1999 compiled by Alice Gray.
Used by permission of Multnomah Publishers, Inc.

The best smell is bread;
the best saver, salt;
the best love, that of children.

George Herbert

Inheritance

It was a beautiful spring morning as we sat at the breakfast table talking about the day before and anticipating the new day at school. Kristen was 10 years old and in the fourth grade, while Ryan was 6 years old and in the first grade.

Kristin was a motivated student and doing well being responsible for her homework and getting ready for school. Mom was complementing Kristen, remarking that as organized as she is she must have Dad's genes. Ryan punctuated the air by saying, "You don't have Dad's 'genes,' I do!"

Since Ryan is our son by adoption, we were puzzling over how we could explain about genes, as sensitively as possible. As we were thinking quickly, Ryan relieved us all by saying, "OK, you can have Dad's jeans, but I've got his T-shirts."

Jeffrey and Martha Comment

Dear Roger
I love You very
much. Yo u are
a neat and
Lovable step
dad to have,
Sometimes
when I have
a bad day
at School
and come home,
You and Mom
make me have
a smile on my
face. from
You step Dauther
Jessica

I AM LOVED

It Comes In Mysterious Ways

A physician is often challenged by a patient's needs, needs that are not met by surgery or medication —tension-easers to get modern man through the modern world. Jogging, alcohol, yoga, acupuncture, sauna, golf, sensitivity sessions, transcendentialing, may all offer special needs. Just sitting, talking, listening are often the wisest course. Then the patient goes home, back into the same routine that has already burdened. Often the physician knows that the real problem is loneliness, an absence of someone caring, a void that could be filled by love. But it is hard to prescribe love, and even harder to get the prescription filled.

When my mother was heavy with child (I like that phrase, it has a frontier, old-days ring), she bought a dog so that upon my arrival, I would have an immediate, steady companion. Now, decades later, I can't imagine life without a doggy buddy. I have had all the problems that come with such a relationship: hair, fleas, rug spots, and pained endings, but the good times have been the reward that I remember. The other things are just a small token, fare for the trip.

Girl dogs, boy dogs, little dogs, big dogs, happy dogs, grumpy dogs, social dogs, finicky dogs. Bullies, cowards, clowns, loafers —I have lived with them all, and we have had good times together. When the time comes, as it does, and my life is without a dog, I develop a strange emptiness, a restlessness, made worse by coming home in the evening without that special kind of greeting.

Getting up in the morning is incomplete without a head to pat. The day is hollow; it echoes; something is missing. The water dish sits empty. The brush, the leash, the flea powder, all goes back into the cupboard. The prescription is obvious. The next canine companion is but a matter of time.

Now, after 50 years of dogged pursuit in trying to understand people and their pressures, I realize that love comes in many forms and disguises, and even mysterious ways.

A dog won't improve the outside world in the least, but for your private moments, he surrounds you with loyalty, happiness, enthusiasm, obedience and affection. Did you ever try to write a prescription with those ingredients?

E. Grey Dimond, M.D.

Love many things, for therein lies the true strength, and whosoever loves much perfoms much, and can accomplish much, and what is done in love is done well.

Vincent Van Gogh

Dear Esuter boney
Pleas leve a prisint
for my mom shy likes
riges, nekle Eose
and pralit.

And cood you get
for my Dad is mony
nov obot millyin dolris.
oh and dont faget
mysiter shy
likes candy
You are a nise buny.
Thank you
P.S.
from
David

Judge Wonderful

I teach foreign language at a prep school, where over the years I have come to realize that the environment of a successful classroom often resembles that of a happy family. I often encourage the students to share baby stories and meaningful events in their lives, and I return in kind. Stories of our daughters, Jill and Jane, and of my husband, who is known to the students as Judge Wonderful, have been a part of what some of my former students have called the "Madame Ulrich Experience."

Not long ago, toward the end of the school day, I was seated at my desk asking the students questions in French over their homework for the day. I was so engaged in this process that I had not realized that our gracious secretary had walked into my classroom, until I glanced up and saw her place a gorgeous arrangement of cut flowers onto my desk. Surprised to be receiving flowers for any reason, I quickly opened the card. All the while, my students were asking questions such as "Madame, who sent you flowers?" or "Madame, is it your birthday, or your anniversary?"

"I don't know, no and no," were my immediate responses. As I opened the card, I read the simple note that said so much. "Just because it's Tuesday, your loving husband." I held the special moment before I looked up at the class and said, "It's from my hubby, Judge Wonderful ... because he loves me and I love him ... and just because it's Tuesday."

Jo Ann Ulrich

Life Lessons From a Coach

There was a high sky on that Saturday. It was a beautiful spring day that was perfect for playing nine innings. I was an assistant baseball coach at Lipscomb University in Nashville. We were 30 minutes away from the first pitch of an important conference game with our rival, Cumberland University.

Batting practice had ended and I had just finished getting the field ready for the game. As another assistant coach began to hit infield, I headed to the coaches' locker room to change into my game uniform. When I got to the locker room, our head coach, Ken Dugan, was finishing dressing for the game.

Coach Dugan was one of the best coaches to ever coach college baseball. He was inducted into five separate halls of fame. He won more than 1,100 games during his career, along with two NAIA national championships and served as an assistant coach for the United States' Pam Am team. On top of that, Coach Dugan authored numerous books and articles. He had multiple chances to take jobs at larger universities, but chose to stay at Lipscomb because he believed in the Christian mission of the university.

While we were dressing in the locker room, we conversed about the upcoming game, but the conversation soon changed directions. I explained to Coach Dugan that recently I had seen a homeless man on the street and had given him a small amount of money. Coach Dugan proceeded to tell me about a time when he gave a homeless man some money and bought him a meal. His voice began to crack as he described the man's reaction. The homeless man thanked Coach Dugan for caring and for spending time with him and then began weeping as he described that no one would look at him or speak to him, much less offer him any help.

As Coach Dugan continued to tell the story, he began to cry. With tears running down his face, he talked about people who discourage others from giving money to homeless people because they will just use the money to buy alcohol and drugs. He said, "How dare people judge the hearts of the homeless. Let the Lord be their judge. If they use the money for drugs and alcohol, then that is between them and the Lord. But that should never stop people from trying to help them."

Coach Dugan had finished dressing. The game would begin in 15 minutes. He wiped his eyes and headed to the field as I finished getting ready. The weight of what had just happened hit me like a ton of bricks. Minutes before a very important game against our biggest rival, one of the most successful coaches in the history of college baseball had just poured out his heart about loving people who are in less fortunate situations. As I walked to the field after getting dressed, I smiled about what had just happened. Very few people who knew Coach Dugan would believe what had just happened. The strict disciplinarian who showed little emotion to his players had just taught his young assistant coach that life and relationships are always more important than your job, even when you are about to play the biggest game of the year.

Kolin Holladay

Editor's Note: Ken Dugan passed away on February 18, 2000. He will always be considered one of the top college baseball coaches in the country.

There is only one happiness in this life, to love and be loved.

George Sand

Love Can Be a Surprise

My wife and I have 10 grandchildren. Arranging alone time with each one isn't always easy, but I do occasionally get some special time with them separately. Whether we go to lunch, go shopping for goodies, or just visit together, it is always time a grandfather treasures.

One day I took one of my 4-year-old grandsons, Jeff, to lunch at his favorite restaurant. We ordered the same grilled hot dogs and french fries we always ordered. We sat happily, side by side, in his favorite booth. As we were eating and chatting away, my grandson spontaneously popped up onto his knees, wrapped his small arms around my neck, and gave me a big, juicy kiss on the cheek. I was surprised but immensely pleased. I looked down at my grandson who had now given his full attention to his french fries. Finally, I said, "Well, thank you, Jeff."

Jeff smiled his beautiful, innocent smile, and we continued eating. A moment later, between bites and swallows, Jeff said, "Do you know why I kissed you, Gramps?" (Jeff asked lots of questions and always wanted to know "why.") Again, my grandson surprised me. I didn't have an answer for him. I replied truthfully, "No, I'm not sure. Why?"

Four-year-old Jeff looked at me with his sparkling, deep, big, brown eyes and said simply without hesitation, "Because I love you." This was all so unexpected, so spontaneous, and so precious that I couldn't speak for a moment. With a lump in my throat, I gave Jeff a hug and a kiss and was able to say without my voice cracking, "Thank you, Jeff. I love you, too."

That experience with my loving grandson was one of the happiest surprises this grandfather has ever had.

Rich Davis

That which we love, we come to resemble.

St Bernard of Clarivaux (French religious)

Love Counts

The doorbell rang. In the doorway, his handsome face brightened with a smile when seeing Marilyn and me. My thoughts left that moment and I pictured the two of us 16 years previously, the same handsome man gently adjusting my new fishing outfit —hat, creel, rod, and all the latest gadgets. There never was a happier 7 year old. The day ended on Electric Lake with fish in the creel and a pat on the head for a job well done! Everywhere we went, people knew my Uncle Buster. What a proud feeling it was to be in his presence.

"Come on, we're going downtown," he said warmly when Marilyn and I opened the door. My thoughts snapped to the present.

"Uncle Bus, I've lots of studying to do. What's going on?" Second-year medical students always had studying to do. His eyes sparkled as he nodded toward the door.

"Marilyn," he said to my new bride, "we'll be right back."

It didn't take us long to reach the medical supply store. "Hi, Buster," said the man in charge. "I have all of the stuff, right here." With that he opened a black physician's bag and produced an otoscope, an ophthalmoscope, and a stethoscope. These were the very tools I would soon need to begin physical diagnosis! Uncle Buster hugged me. We both wiped a tear from our eyes. There never was a happier 23-year-old.

Uncle Buster loved and was loved. He made everyone feel wonderful. Always thoughtful and never without a smile. Come visit sometime. I'll show you my fishing rod and black bag.

Stanley N. Stark, M.D.

*The most important things to do in the world
are to get something to eat,
something to drink
and somebody to love you.*

Brandan Behan

Love in the Factory

I first met Charles while we were working on the line at a large factory. Charles and I were from very different backgrounds.

Charlie grew up as the son of a black sharecropper in Louisiana. There were 17 children in his family and you were expected to start working in the field at the age of 4. According to Charlie, his mother would have a baby and be back in the field working in three days. Charlie is lucky to be walking. At the age of 8, he was diagnosed with polio. With his big sister's encouragement, he recovered and learned to walk again. Charlie went on to be the only one in his family to graduate from college.

When I first met Charlie, he was cautious of me. We were of a different race and I appeared to be a little too ambitious. We started working next to each other on the assembly line and our original preconception of each other faded away. Even though we were two very different people from two very different backgrounds with very different ambitions, we became close friends.

One day I got word that I was being promoted and moved to another department. Charlie left me a note. He told me that our time together had meant a great deal to him. He said he loved me like a brother and that he would never forget our time working together. He said he was sad because he knew that we would drift apart and our friendship would end. I told Charlie that I would never forget him and that we would always be friends. He was skeptical. I told him that I never let my friendships die.

It's been more than 15 years since we first met, and neither one of us work for the same company anymore. Charlie is a schoolteacher and I am the president of my own company. We are still friends. He since has told me that he knew our friendship would never end. Me, too.

Rick Krska

Just don't give up trying to do what you really want to do. Where there is love and inspiration, I don't think you can go wrong.

Ella Fitzgerald, American Singer

HUGS

It's wondrous what a hug can do,
A hug can cheer you when you're blue,
A hug can say, "I love you so."
Or, "Gee! I hate to see you go."

A hug is, "Welcome back again!"
And, "It's great to see you!"
"Where have you been?"
A hug can soothe a small child's pain
And bring a rainbow after the rain.

The HUG! There's just no doubt about it,
We scarcely could survive without it.
A hug delights, warms and charms,
It must be why God gave us arms.

Hugs are great for fathers and mothers.
Sweet for sister, swell for brothers,
And chances are some favorite aunts
Love them more than potted plants.

Kittens crave them. Puppies love them,
Heads of state are not above them.
A hug can break the language barrier,
And make the dullest day seem merrier.

No need to fret about the store of 'em,
The more you give, the more there are of 'em.
So stretch those arms without delay,
And give someone a HUG today!

Author Unknown

Love is a Granddaughter

We have nine grandchildren, all of whom live considerable distance from us. We did, however, enjoy the pleasure and the thrill of having our 4-year-old granddaughter spend an entire week with us (without her parents!).

She was a perfect angel for the entire stay, never feeling lonely for her mother or dad, who she loves dearly and to whom she spoke throughout her visit. She never cried nor did we ever require a "time-out" for improper behavior.

At the airport, she hugged and kissed us goodbye. We put her on the plane (with our housekeeper) for her return trip to Seattle.

Upon her arriving home she had her dad phone us. She got on the telephone to tell us what a "great time" she had, and how much she missed us. She said she was looking forward to another visit in Los Angeles "real sooon"!

When our housekeeper returned to our home, she told us that our granddaughter cried for 20 minutes without letting up! She made such a scene, that while taxiing for the take-off, the stewardess volunteered to return to the gate. Come to find out, she was crying because she wanted to stay with her Nanny and Poppa "O."

How's that for feeling loved?

Cydney & Bill Osterman

Dear Mommy,
This brings a speial wish for you,
When Mother's Day is here
And lots of hugs and kisses
Enough to last all year.
I love you becaus you make
good muffins. Love Lisa

Love Never Dies

My mother died of metastasized breast cancer in May of 1998. My father died essentially of a broken heart one and a half years later. I was able to be with them during the last months of their lives, which I consider to be the most profound and enriching experience of my life. I was born in the middle of the 20th century, and for 50 years I was nurtured by the love my parents gave me. I may not have been very successful, I may not have always done what they expected of me, but I never once felt their love waiver.

Because they loved me, I have been able to give love to others. That is how it works. Because I loved them, I was able to be a part of their passing. Their love gave me strength, and it still does today. The truth is … love never dies … it is a power greater than we are that grows as it is given.

Kathryn Callaway Sullivan

*Tis better to have loved and lost,
than never to have loved at all.*

Alfred Lord Tennyson

to Daddy
I Love you
xoxo

Dad
We all
Love you.
We are
Glad God
gave
us you.

Love Was Least Expected

I have always lived by the saying, "You can't judge a book by its cover." As human beings, unfortunately we often forget to practice what we preach. So when I first met Michael Mazza, I thought that we would become as close as oil and water.

Michael had just been released from jail on bond a few days before I met him. I have never been around someone who had been arrested because I was always told "those" were not the proper kind of people to be around. In fact, people who had been arrested can actually only get you into trouble, or so I had been told.

Due to mutual friends, Michael and I slowly began to hang out together and go surfing. For a few weeks we remained acquaintances and talked to each other regularly.

Then my world was shattered due to family problems. Because of these problems, for the first time in my life I felt completely alone. Yet no matter what, Michael was there for me and would listen while I cried on his shoulder.

One day I was having an especially hard day. Out of the blue, Michael turned to me and said "Beth Ann, I hate to see you so upset. You are my best friend and it hurts me to see you this upset."

His statement, that he said so nonchalantly, meant more to me than any other thing that has been said to me by any of my friends, because looking into his big, warm brown eyes, I realized that he truly meant it from his heart.

Beth Ann Holzclaw

With ♥ Love !!

Jeremy !!

Get well soon
Uncle John

Love Survives

Our young son had misbehaved one day. While I was discussing it with him, he threw a full-blown tantrum saying things like, "I don't like you anymore!" and "I don't want to live with you."

Later, after he calmed down, he came to me and said, "Mommy, you know I love you. Even when I'm mad, I love you, and even if I say I don't like you, I love you. And when I say I don't want to live with you anymore, remember I don't mean it."

I turned to him with tears in my eyes and gave him the biggest hug saying, "You know I always love you, too." That afternoon turned out to be one of the highlights of being a parent for me.

Jessica Rudnick-Kaseff

Wicked men obey from fear; good men, from love.

Aristotle

To Mother

Happy Mother's Day

Love Shelley

Love, New Orleans Style

I grew up in New Orleans in a large extended family that has always enjoyed just "hanging out" together. Granted, I should preface this by saying that I don't want to paint a picture of the perfect family because, trust me, we have our dysfunctions just like many other families. But, we love to laugh, have fun and just do whatever. Anytime I come back after a trip home, people will ask me what I did there, thinking that with a fairly famous family we must have done something extravagant. My usual answer is, "We just hung out together and laughed."

Even though it hasn't always been a picture-perfect setting, we all have a deep love for each other, and we enjoy being together regardless of what we're doing. (And there's no telling what's going to happen.) We kind of travel in packs because it's fun. Whenever we know we're going to be together, we start calling each other ahead of time to make arrangements to meet at the movies, or plan to go to the mall, or plan to do whatever together. It's a great feeling to know that we care for each other that much.

Anytime we talk to each other, any of us, we always say "I love you" before hanging up the phone. To me, that's nice.

In our family, I was always taught to love people for who they are. It doesn't matter what they do for a living, what they don't do for a living, what color their skin is, or whatever differences and similarities we might have ... people are people and you should see them from the heart. I was taught to see people as if my eyes are the tools, but I'm looking with my heart. That's it. You can love people by smiling at them. I always say "hi" to people, even strangers, because a simple smile can make that person's day. That's a way to give love. A general "hello," holding the door open, or some other generic, simple act of kindness is, I think, a wonderful way to spread love.

Arthel Neville

Editor's Note: Arthel, currently an anchor on the FOX News Channel, is the daughter of Art Neville of the Grammy award-winning Neville Brothers. Her mother is Doris Neville. When asked about the size of her extended family, Arthel replied, "As we say in New Orleans, 'beau coup'!"

When you arise in the morning, think of what a precious privilege it is to be alive to breathe, to think, to enjoy, to love.

Marcus Aurelius

Loving Ladd

The diagnosis came in December, before Christmas. Our friend, Ladd, had melanoma, a fast-growing cancer so virulent that her doctor went to her home to deliver the news.

Our little group that had been meeting for seven years moved to begin a 12-month period of focusing on supporting our friend. Countless others joined in. Some were strangers. When Ladd became increasingly homebound, someone learned of her interest in watching birds, and placed feeders strategically at her windows.

Ladd demonstrated a delight in small events. She told us about a conversation with her 5-year-old granddaughter who also had a birdfeeder. Ladd asked her granddaughter if she'd seen any sparrows? Her granddaughter gravely replied, "Yes, I've seen asparagus birds." So during one of her hospital stays, we decorated her room with "asparagus birds," chains of green construction paper ones. We also made posters for the hospital walls and met in the chapel to pray for her. One member gave Ladd manicures.

We sent notes to encourage. We brought her Foo's custard, one of her favorite foods. And always, we continued to include her in our weekly meetings. When she weakened, we drove her. When she was not able to get out, we met at her house. And when she was too ill to meet, we doubled our efforts to stay connected and available.

Our last time with Ladd took place on a cold and gray December afternoon. We gathered around her bed, held her hands, and told her we loved her. Then we moved to a corner of her bedroom and quietly prayed, first expressing our thanks for the opportunity to encircle her, and second with a request for her release.

Two days later, she was gone, leaving a powerful legacy. Ladd graciously let many love her. And all who had the privilege are better for it.

Julie Zimmer

When you put faith, hope and love together, you can raise positive kids in a negative world.

Zig Ziglar

Marilyn

My story is about Marilyn, a principal at an elementary school. It has been several years since Marilyn passed away. Still, I haven't been able to stop thinking about the love and caring that she showed to her students and teachers while she was with us.

Marilyn found out that she had a terminal form of cancer the week before my younger daughter, Bailey, started kindergarten. It had been Marilyn's dream to be a principal at that elementary school, and she had been eager to start the school year. I don't know how she felt when she learned that her tenure at the school would be cut short, but she behaved like nothing was out of the ordinary. Those few who knew about her condition thought that she must have received a medical report that we had not heard about. We didn't think that she could care for each of the children and the teachers in the way that she did if she knew it was going to be taken away from her so quickly.

How would you describe Marilyn's way? It was individual attention to each child's and teacher's needs. Bailey was having trouble separating from home early in the school year and cried for the first 20 or 30 minutes of every day. Marilyn observed this and asked Bailey if it would help if she met her at the school's front door and walked her to class. Bailey said that would help a lot, and Marilyn was as good as her word. For weeks, she met Bailey at the front door and walked her to her classroom. Bailey's fears about going to school eased, and her crying stopped.

In another instance, a couple of the teachers had problems teaching certain subjects or handling some of their students. Marilyn learned about their problems and spent lots of time in those teachers' classrooms, observing their work. At the end of each class, she sat with the teacher and made suggestions about different ways to approach the subject or the student.

Marilyn's philosophy seemed to be that no student or teacher was a lost cause. If the student or teacher wanted to improve themselves, Marilyn believed they could do so. She also seemed to feel that the most important thing in the world was helping that student or teacher to accomplish whatever they were trying to accomplish. At her funeral, I learned that Marilyn had not been a good high school student. She had been told that she was not college material, but she didn't believe it. She worked hard at her studies because she knew that her natural talents would not be enough for her to reach her goal of becoming a teacher. Her perseverance paid off, and she became a teacher.

I never learned how she or why she made the switch from teacher to school principal, but from my vantage point, it was the perfect use of her talents. Marilyn was whatever the moment required of her: friend, coach, administrator, loving parent, under-standing counselor, and even disciplinarian — although that last role must have been more difficult for her to play than the others.

During Marilyn's second year at the school, her

strength ebbed and her absences became more frequent. In April, an acting-principal was named and Marilyn was unable to return to school after that. In mid-July, we heard that the end was very near. A week later, she passed away.

The church that held her funeral was filled with students, teachers and townspeople. A couple of Marilyn's close friends read notes that students and teachers had sent during her final months. The students' notes were filled with stories of little things that Marilyn had done for them or said to them. In every note, the underlying message was "Your actions and your words showed me that you cared about me, and it was important for me to know that."

The teachers' notes were a little different. Those notes were about difficult problems that the teachers had experienced in the classroom. None of the problems lent themselves to quick solutions. Marilyn, however, had been willing to put in the time to help these teachers over their hurdles. In the process, she changed the way they viewed their work. Initially, each of them was surprised that Marilyn considered their problems important enough to devote the time and effort that she did to make them more effective teachers. Later, when they realized that Marilyn knew how limited her remaining time was, they were flattered and embarrassed that she had chosen to spend that time helping them to become better teachers. Marilyn had shown them through her actions just how important it was for them to do their jobs as well as they could.

The last part of the funeral service was electrifying,

at least for me. The speaker announced that in closing, they would play recordings of some of Marilyn's favorite music. I don't remember what songs were played, but Amazing Grace was probably one of them. All I remember was that as the music played, I sensed Marilyn's spirit in the room. I thought to myself, "I know why I'm feeling this." In my own daughters, I could sense the love that Marilyn had shown them. A number of the teachers had the same look in their eyes that Marilyn had when she was determined to do something.

Marilyn was gone, but through her love and determination, she had passed on her spirit to a group in that room who would carry it on.

H. Joseph Price, Jr.

You love simply because you cannot help it.

Unknown

Memento of Love

My late husband was a very thoughtful, generous man during our almost 58 years of marriage. As a result, I have many beautiful mementos.

On my birthday in 1987, Will gave me a coin-shaped gold pendant on a chain. The back of it was engraved from him to me with the date. In bold print is "I Am Loved." For almost nine years this has been around my neck —always showing, always cherished. A constant reminder of our lasting love.

Margaret Harsh

The hunger for love is much more difficult to remove than the hunger for bread.

Mother Teresa

I love my famly
My teacher she is my mom
she teachis me things that
I injoy it I love her vere
much she is my dream come
troo

Linda

Meeting Andrew

In 1967, things were different than they are today. I was different. It is hard to believe, being who I am today, that I didn't stand up to my parents and keep Andrew. But I had never been away from home and was totally dependent on my parents. We were all very dependent on what others thought. And having a child out of wedlock was not done in our town in those days. So when I became pregnant, I was shipped off to my grandparents who lived on the Illinois River near Peoria, Ill. for six months or so.

The night I gave birth to Andrew is still so vivid in my mind. I begged not to have to give him up. I held that little baby and would have done anything to keep him, but I didn't know how to do anything. Literally. So I signed the papers and handed him back to the nurse. That was the last I heard about that child but not the last I thought about him. Mom and Dad took care of all of the adoption arrangements.

No joyous celebrations when I got home. No hugs. No counseling. There was NEVER any mention of this child I had born or what I might have gone through. I knew nothing of what happened to him after I held him. It was a family secret. I kept it hidden, too.

In 1998, when Andrew was 28, he went to the agency where his parents adopted him in Peoria and asked about finding his birth mother. They told him to think hard about it as it could turn out very bad. He went away for two years and contemplated if he was ready for any circumstance. He returned to the agency in the spring of 2000 and said he felt he was prepared for anything. So the search began.

It didn't take long for the caseworker to find my father who, at 86, still lives in the same town, and had the same phone number. Being very careful not to say why she was calling, the caseworker asked for Dad, who, in turn, gave her my phone number.

She called my home and left me a message. I returned the call, not knowing who I was calling. It was my hometown area code, so I thought it was an old friend. I left a message for her, but somehow it wasn't received. Luckily, the caseworker didn't give up. She got my e-mail address from Dad. When I saw her e-mail, I started to cry. I knew what it was. It was all those painful memories that I'd buried 30 years ago and had not allowed myself to think about.

I called her the next morning. I was so excited to find out that he was looking for me. She began to tell me a little bit about Andrew. It was so wonderful to hear that he had wonderful parents and had grown up to become a nice person. The caseworker said reunions like this is why she does her job. Andrew and I were both so excited about meeting each other. I gave her all my contact information and said to let Andrew contact me as he wished.

When I got to work later that day, I had the first e-mail from him.

I immediately went and got a book on adoptive reunions. It was very helpful. That weekend, my son whom I raised, Jonathan, was able to come up from

Arkansas where he lives. It helped having him around because I couldn't even get dressed I was so depressed. I had to relive it all those months at my grandparents, the shame of friends and family, the birth, the pain of giving him up, the pain of not knowing. All the pain and suffering I had gone through all those years. And I had to adjust to the fact that it was NOT a secret anymore. Friends were bringing me "It's a Boy" balloons and such.

I told Jonathan when he was 18 (he's 27 now) about Andrew. For the past nine years, he has wanted me to find his brother, but I didn't even know that there was an agency involved, since the arrangements had all been taken care of for me.

I was afraid to talk to Andrew on the phone or even see him. Then I was driving to work about five days after finding out about him and something clicked. I needed to meet this child of mine. The next day I went to meet Andrew, his wife, his mom and dad, and his friends. My father and my significant other came with me to meet everyone. Andrew's mom and dad are wonderful. We shared stories and the boy's baby books. It was a tough but wonderful weekend.

Jonathan also has gone home to meet Andrew and his family. It has healed a lot for Andrew and Jonathan. They don't look too much alike but they act alike. They grew up doing the same stuff skateboarding, music, black leather jackets, long hair. Also, their hands are just alike I think that is so cool.

In the beginning, Andrew and I agreed to try to not have any expectations, which has helped. We have a very good relationship. We e-mail a few times a week.

Andrew and his wife have moved to my hometown and are both working at the firm where my father worked for 41 years.

It's amazing to think that after all these years, and trying to not think about him, that I still am loved. So is he.

Cheryl Hanback

A bell isn't a bell until you ring it
A song isn't a song until you sing it
And love wasn't put in your heart to stay
Love isn't love until you give it away.

Unknown

Mother-In-Love

When I think of love, my dear 92-year-old mother-in-law comes immediately to mind. She has set a constant example of love shining through her soul for the 43 years her son and I have been married. It always amazes me to hear friends tell their mother-in-law horror stories. To me, it seems so right to have "another Mom."

As a bride and then as an inexperienced new mother, I can only remember her helping me in a thoughtful kind way rather than a critical way. We were visiting her one weekend with our first infant who was crying loudly in the night. I was up with him, myself about to cry in desperation. She came out of her bedroom, blurry-eyed and quickly figured out there was a problem with the bottle. She performed a quiet miracle before my eyes. What I remember most about this incident was her calm, positive way of handling the situation instead of being critical.

I still have the 1953 edition of the Betty Crocker cookbook that she gave me, knowing that she thought her son might not survive on the tuna fish on toast that I was regularly preparing. The tuna was so thick it actually stuck to the plate! But, again, instead of being critical she graciously handled the situation in a loving and sincere way.

Recently she told me I was a gift from God to her because she always wanted a daughter. I think of her as a gift from God to me. I am so lucky to have two loving moms.

Now that I am a mother-in-law and grandmother, I try to remember to be quietly positive with my children's spouses and let love and respect shine through.

Beverly Deming

We can do no great things only small things with great love.

Mother Teresa

Mother

I used to wonder why she stood there
Softly, in my bedroom doorway;
Often, I would start, awakening
To her silent smile.

Suddenly, I know her reason
As I stand in my son's doorway
Gazing silently, and feeling
No boundaries to my love.

Joan King Holtzman

Mrs. Haley

While I was the city manager of Dallas, my secretary, periodically for the first several years, would come in my office and say, "Mrs. Haley told me to tell you to forget about the…" and then continue with whatever issue or critique we may have been dealing with. For seven years, I never directly spoke to Mrs. Haley. She was an older lady who was proper and dignified, and went to the council meetings to simply watch. She never said anything. Often she'd call the office and have my secretary give me some type of message of encouragement, but she never would talk to me directly.

One time, my secretary, Ms. Pitts, came in and said, "Mrs. Haley called and said, 'Would you tell my city manager that I would really appreciate it if he would send me a Christmas card.'" Even though I had not met her, I sent her a Christmas card. Mrs. Haley called my secretary and asked her to thank me for the card. My plan was to send her a card the next year without her calling. Guess what I did … I forgot to send her a card. She called Ms. Pitts and asked if "my city manager will send me a Christmas card."

This type of exchange went on for seven years. I finally went out and met her. Come to find out, Mrs. Haley lived with her sister, and she was the telephone operator at an old hotel here in town. Occasionally, I would drop by and see her. And she continued to call the office, but never talked to me directly because she didn't want to bother me.

When I retired from the city, I called her and said, "Mrs. Haley, I want you to come to my office." I brought her into the office and had the city photographer come by and take her picture. We put it in a frame and sent it to her. Over the years, that strange association became deeper and bigger. I would go to her house every Christmas and take them fruit or flowers, and just visit with them. They called me at the hospital during my wife's sickness to tell me they were offering prayers every night for her.

Mrs. Haley got sick and was terminally ill. Her sister called and said how Mrs. Haley's niece was awfully distraught because Mrs. Haley didn't have long to live, and they didn't know if she had enough money for a proper funeral service. She had a cemetery plot and a $1,000 burial policy, but they didn't think that would cover it. They were calling me to see if I had any suggestions of what they could do. I said, "You tell Mrs. Haley that I'll take care of it and she'll have a proper service." She died a short time after that and we had about six of us that went out and sat around the coffin while the minister provided graveside service.

Our relationship was one of great affection from what started out to be total strangers, into a second-hand association that developed over seven years. It went from never meeting, to a good friendship with Mrs. Haley and her sister. I will always remember Mrs. Haley.

George Schrader

My Best Friend

In the summer of 1992, I longed to return to Colorado and revive memories of my early teaching days in Canyon City. Since my spouse was unable to take time from her work, I decided to invite my son, Kurt.

Kurt responded with a "Yes!"

The more I thought about it, the more I felt it would be important for him to take a good friend. "You plan the trip and I'll just go for the ride." He declined the offer to take a friend but agreed to plan the route of the trip.

We had a wonderful time, stopping at every comic book store between McPherson, Kan. and the western slopes of the Colorado Rocky Mountains. Arriving back at McPherson, I helped Kurt unload and proceeded to leave. He came to the car and I rolled down the window. "Dad, you told me that I could take a good friend. I want you to know I took my best friend."

The tears streamed from my face as I drove away. He had given me enough love for a lifetime.

Bud Cooper

My Significant Influence — An Essay

In life everyone gets born into a family and they are stuck with that family whether they like that family or not. As for me, I like my family, especially my grandmother who has taught me never give up and anything is possible. My grandmother, Betty, married my grandfather, Richard. He died when I was only 3 years old. It still makes me a little sad, but he is still with me in a recurring dream I have about playing on a playground.

My grandmother does not bake me cookies. She does not knit me socks. My grandmother is of a different breed. Instead she takes me to Jamaica, Mexico, Japan; she sends me to the Caribbean for a month, takes me to her yoga class and goes to Pearl Jam concerts. What is even more amazing is that she is the Mayor of the most affluent city in Kansas, Mission Hills. I grew up going to city council meetings and discussing what Mission Hills should do about its flood-lands. We are going to see the world together, for us there is no time to bake.

When my parents divorced when I was 10 years old, and my brother was 12, she was our biggest advocate. She worked diligently to save my older brother and I. She would take us out to dinner and we had sleepovers in her house. Even way past our bedtimes, it was not odd to find us dancing around to Jimmy Buffet's "Songs You Know by Heart." She made me forget about my parents. I love my grandmother all the way to Pluto and back.

Last October, she took my brother and I out to brunch. It was very nice. Then, we went back to her house and she sat us down on the couch. She told us that she had breast cancer. My heart plunged 15 stories down past my toes. I cried for three days and three nights. She was having surgery the next day and would be in the hospital for a week. I went to visit her every day. She did not smoke, she only ate organic foods and she did yoga. How could this have happened to my grandmother when she was supposed to be immortal?

She got better, the cancer was in remission and everything was fine. Fine enough in fact for her to take us all to Puerto Vallarta, Mexico for the millennium. Then, in February she told us that she had colon cancer. She had surgery and the doctors took out 1/5 of her colon. Even when she was in the hospital, she wanted to know about my problems. She is fine now, getting ready for the Pearl Jam concert next week.

My truly amazing grandmother has taught me that I should not be afraid to fall in love, age is only a number that measures how long you have lived-not how much fun you are allowed to have and family comes first.

Elyse Rohrer

When I was one-and-twenty
I heard him say again,
The heart out of the bosom
Was never given in vain;
'Tis paid with sighs a plenty
And sold for endless rue',
And I am two-and-twenty,
And oh, 'tis true, 'tis true.

A.E. Housman

Dear Dad
I hope you
have a very
happy
valentine's
Love Love
Love   Ann

One Quick Deal

When I was working in Los Angeles, a close friend asked me to come and have lunch with him and his father at the poolside of the hotel where they were staying. After lunch we walked around the pool and he introduced me to several of his friends, one of which was an attractive young lady named Lois. For the next year, Lois and I saw each other occasionally at restaurants or parties and were always cordial, but we never dated.

About a year later, my father became ill and as part of his recovery, wanted to go to California. He asked me to accompany him and be his driver and helper. In the evenings I escorted my father and mother to restaurants, but usually before 6:00 p.m. to avoid the crowds.

During that period, another friend called me and said, "I am having an engagement party tonight at the Ambassador Hotel and Harry Belafonte is opening at the Coconut Grove. Please join me and bring a date." I said I appreciated the invitation but I have to be with my father. He said, "Nevertheless, if it works out, see if you can join the party."

At dinner that evening, my father said he was really tired and asked me to take him home after dinner and that I could go out and do whatever I wanted. On the way out of the restaurant, in came Lois with her mother, father and brother. My exact words to her were, "Lois, I will give you one quick deal. Harry Belafonte is opening at the Coconut Grove and a friend of mine is having a party there tonight. Would you like to go out?"

She said, "It's my mother's birthday, let me ask." Her parents said it was all right and for me to come back after dinner to pick her up. I did. We were engaged three weeks later and have been married for more than 40 years. She never realized how "one quick deal" could lead to a lifetime love affair!

By the way, several years later Lois told me she really wasn't so interested in going out with me that night as much as she wanted to see Harry Belafonte!

Tom Davidson

Love turns one person into two;
and two into one.

Isaac Abravanel

Phone Tag

It all started, strangely enough, at an Orlando Cubs baseball game. I went there alone, looking for a distraction while in the middle of a painful divorce. As sometimes happens at these things, I spent part of the game visiting with a perfect stranger, talking baseball and who knows what else, and never thinking twice about it. He left for a better seat in the seventh inning, and I went home after the last out.

Fast-forward two months to July of 1995. I began receiving messages at work to call a woman whose name I didn't recognize, at a phone number and area code that were also foreign to me. Since I worked as a reporter for an Orlando radio station, I thought it was just a PR person trying to get a story on the air, so I returned the call, and we played phone tag for several days until finally, Rebecca Rourk got me.

"Do you remember going to a baseball game a few weeks ago?" she asked me.

"Yes," I replied.

"Do you remember talking with someone there?"

"Sure."

"Well, he's a friend of mine, we used to date, and he told me I should call you because we both have a lot in common!"

Now, that REALLY got my attention! I laughed, told her it sounded interesting, and asked if I could call her back that night, when we could both talk a little longer and with a little more privacy. And by the way, where WAS she calling from?

"Kansas City!" she said.

"What are you doing there?"

"I live here!"

"Oh, great, " I thought. Not only a fix-up...but one from halfway across the country. Still, there was a warmth, a certain quality to her voice and personality that made me think this was likely to be better than the average blind date from hell.

I only slightly underestimated what would happen. Neither one of us had anything to lose; the ice had already been broken, so there was no awkward beginning to our conversation. And what a conversation it was. We talked about everything from our past relationships to music, movies, TV (especially "Seinfeld"). We talked about animals (I have two cats and she's an animal lover), and about my career as a starving journalist and hers as a successful copywriter for a design studio (and that she was not bothered by the fact that she made more money than I). By the time we were ready to wrap it up, three hours had gone by, it was approaching midnight (my time) and we agreed to continue the next night (THAT conversation was an abbreviated two hours!). By then, I fully realized I might have found that special someone who had eluded me for so long.

With the first two nights under our belt, we agreed on two ground rules. The first, in order to keep from going bankrupt, was to place a half-hour limit on our phone calls. The second was not to send each other our pictures, just yet. Appropriately enough for a radio guy, the early days of this relationship would be based on voice and the written word, not pictures and appearances. We caved in on the pictures after three weeks, although Rebecca had sent me a childhood photo to show me she was a natural blonde.

I can't tell you how often we wrote in those pre-email days, I think it was almost every day. I couldn't wait to get home to see what was in the mailbox. I couldn't wait to finish each letter or card to mail to Rebecca.

We spoke every night, no matter where we were. After three weeks, I told her I loved her…and she told me the same, sight mostly unseen.

We finally met when, serendipitously, I was invited to my cousin's wedding in…. Kansas City! I was so low on funds; my brother bought me a plane ticket as a birthday present. He knew all about what was going on, and he also knew I was happier than I'd been in a long time. Rebecca and I had about three weeks to get nervous, and get over getting nervous, but I'll tell you, I'd never been so nervous in my life as I was when I flew out there. I think I spent a half-hour in the restroom on the plane making sure every hair was in place and my breath was perfect!

Rebecca was at the airport to meet me with flowers, wine, and a chauffeured Lincoln Town Car, and my first words to her were, "You're even more beautiful than your picture!" I was so thrilled to finally see her, I nearly left the airport without my luggage!

That Friday turned out to be the most romantic day of my life, and while I had to leave her for my family obligations that night, we were back together for a 24-

hour marathon of movies, talk and romance Sunday and Monday. It was only the beginning of what became a year-long love affair from a distance, with me flying to Kansas City, Rebecca flying to Orlando, or the two of us flying to New York every few weeks to be together. Her first visit to Orlando came three weeks after we first met … and the fact that she hit it off with my cats, Zeke and Gremlin, clinched it for me! In between visits, there were the daily phone calls, sometimes several of them every day. We watched "Seinfeld" and other TV shows together from a distance.

There were hundreds of letters, cards and care packages. AT&T, the airlines and the Postal Service must have loved us! Most important, we loved each other, and spoke of when it would always be "our time."

That came the following summer; Rebecca made the big move to Orlando, giving up her job in Kansas City. Here would be the true test of our relationship. She stayed with me until finding a job, then moved into her own place (she wanted her own space, and I didn't mind a bit). Rebecca put up with my baseball, I put up with her Martha Stewart, and we both enjoyed the things we loved, together.

Several times I asked her to marry me, but it was never a serious enough moment for her to say "yes." "How can I take you seriously when you're sitting around in your shorts?" she'd ask. She finally said, "Yes," one August afternoon as we enjoyed coffee and snacks at our favorite hangout, a used bookstore and café in Orlando's College Park section.

Since then, we've been through some tough times, the illnesses of our mothers, the death of our beloved cat, Zeke. We've also been through some exhilarating times, including the building of our home, and wonderful vacations in London, the Carribean and New York. We had a wonderfully non-traditional wedding (so much of our relationship has been unconventional, why start now?). But most importantly, we're there for each other day in and day out, even when I'm on the road for my work.

Our favorite activity is just "hanging out" at home with our cats, Gremlin and Shadow (who we adopted several months after Zeke died). We enjoy reading, TV, movies, music, and sometimes, just doing nothing. After all, the true test of a relationship is knowing that two people just enjoy being with each other!

Peter King Steinhaus

Editor's Note: Peter King, as he is known on the air, is no longer a "starving jour-nalist." Now he is an anchor and reporter for CBS News Radio, and he writes for "Radio World," a broadcast industry publication. Rebecca is (as Peter puts it) a "successful and enormously creative copywriter" for the "Orlando Sentinel" news-paper.

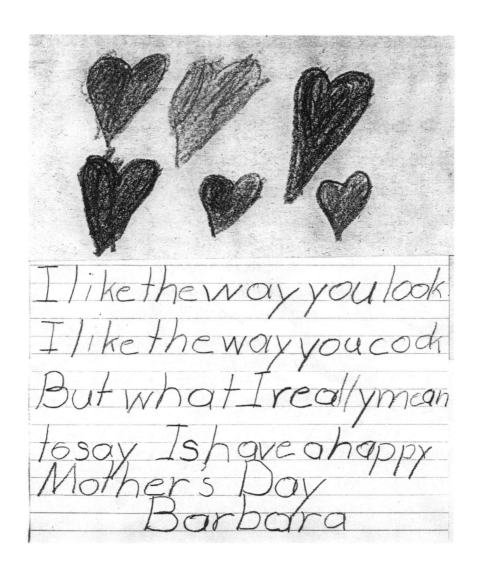

I like the way you look
I like the way you cook
But what I really mean
to say Is have a happy
Mother's Day
Barbara

You've got to sing
like you don't need the money.
You've got to love
like you'll never get hurt.
You've got to dance
like there's nobody watching.
You've got to come from the heart,
if you want it to work.

Susanna Clark

Saturday Afternoon

My grandmother (I called her "Mom") played an important role in my life. My mother worked, so "Mom" picked me up and took me home for an after school treat and chat. Talking was easy with this tall woman with beautiful white hair and blue eyes that always seemed to sparkle with kindness and reflect her love of life. She inspired confidence. I felt I could tell her anything and knew she'd be there for me, no matter what the problem.

Our most special time together was the unvarying Saturday ritual. My grandmother, mother and I always spent the afternoon together. We'd have lunch and go shopping. A simple treat, but so very special to me. I always looked forward to Saturdays!

Then everything changed. My beloved "Mom" — source of love, strength and just plain fun— developed Alzheimer's. At first forgetful, then incoherent, she eventually stopped talking and no longer recognized us. The relentless process continued for 10 years, and my Saturday visits were now to the home she'd entered as her condition slowly deteriorated. Mumbles replaced her insightful comments, and my smiles were often forced as I sat on the bed trying to coax a return smile, a few words, some acknowledgment that my presence even mattered!

One day, at the end of this new Saturday ritual, I

was feeling particularly useless. All the hundreds of visits were for what? She didn't even know me. I kissed her good-bye, wondering where "Mom" really was and if she knew how much I cared, how I missed her. Then it happened. She grabbed my arm, looked up at me with again-familiar blue eyes and said, quite clearly, "I love you."

Never again did I doubt the rightness of continuing our Saturday afternoon ritual.

Jeanne Sheehy

*"When one loves somebody,
everything is clear—
where to go, what to do—
it all takes care of itself."*

Maxim Gorky

Say It with a Kiss

My grandparents, Charles and Pearl, were married for 58 years. The earliest memories I have of them have remained consistent. Always rock solid and envied for the love and respect they had for each other and for all human beings. With a pure goodness, they influenced our family, their friends and the scores of bystanders that crossed their path throughout a very full lifetime they shared together.

From 1943-1945, Charles Esensten battled the Japanese in the Pacific Ocean, leaving behind his wife, their two babies, and his four brothers for her to raise. He was captain of a landing ship tank carrier. Every night before he went to sleep and every morning when he would rise, Chuck kissed the photograph of my grandmother that he kept next to his bed. Then he would pray to God to bring him safely home.

Today my grandpa often tells this tale while showing the same photo of Grandma that he had during the War. That photo now rests on the nightstand in their Los Angeles home. He refers to his beloved Pearl as "the love of my life, my beautiful wife" —even now that she is gone.

After having been subjected to two years of war and loneliness, my grandparents made a pact that anytime my grandpa would leave the house, they would kiss each other goodbye. I witnessed this public display of commitment and love throughout every stage of my life.

Chuck and Pearl understood the importance of a kiss and the magnitude of a moment that might be their last. My grandparents passed on this jewel for me to treasure ... A kiss, short and sweet or long and passionate, always speaks louder than words.

Suzanne Fenton

Of all forms of caution,
caution in love is perhaps
the most fatal to true happiness.

Bertrand Russell

Sense of Duty

It's hard for me to believe that I would be so inspired by the work of a Hollywood director, but I left Steven Spielberg's film, "Saving Private Ryan," in complete awe and with many questions. Why did the Allied soldiers depicted in the invasion of Normandy keep going in the face of the intensity of German artillery? We are shown that the losses were immense and as the troops invaded, their comrades were actually mowed down around them. Why did they keep going?

It finally dawned on me that they did it out of sense of duty. Dedication to honor. But mostly, I think, they fought for love: of their country, of their family, and for all those who were not yet born. It struck me then that they kept going for me.

I don't think that the generation into which I was born has truly experienced the kind of commitment displayed in the film. A belief or love so strong that, without question, one would lay down their life for another human. We have been well protected by those who did. For the first time in my life, I caught a glimpse, an understanding to some degree, of what their sacrifices were, and I am honored that they were made for me.

Patrice Eilts-Jobe

Sharing the Wealth

Love is sharing the wealth of another human being. I do not mean money or possessions. I mean the treasure of knowing another human being. My husband and I have the good fortune of loving each other and our six children. We pray that by showing our children they are safely loved within our family, that they will carry that love into the greater community of life. Just think of the endless good fortune and wealth they will have from sharing the wealth of loving relationships. One of our children wrote a poem about love and I would like to share it.

Mundanity

How can our minds remain intact?
Or, for that matter, sane?
If the greatest beauty, love
Were to become mundane.

Just cycles, thoughts, and common things
Such magic cannot be
It must not be set with an average day
Or any anomaly

In a world where all is accepted
Even miracles have their place

Can't we keep a bit of sympathy
For a loved one's heart or face?

Granted, we must all preserve
Love's nature's simplicity
In a world of logic mundanity
By its power we are free.

Andy Nelson, 12/5/96

Joanie Brody

"I've always taught that love and balance are the two most important things. Love is the most important and the second is balance."

John Wooden

I LoVe
you
More
than this

Love is a Grandparent

A preschooler who lives down the street was curious about grandparents. It occurred to me that, to a child, grandparents appear like an apparition with no explanation, no job description and few credentials. They just seem to go with the territory.

This, then, is for the little folks who wonder what a grandparent is.

A grandparent can always be counted on to buy all your cookies, flower seeds, all-purpose greeting cards, transparent tape, paring knives, peanut brittle and ten chances on a pony. (Also a box of taffy when they have dentures.)

A grandparent helps you with the dishes when it is your night.

A grandparent is the only baby-sitter who doesn't charge more after midnight —or anything before midnight.

A grandparent buys you gifts your mother says you don't need.

A grandparent arrives three hours early for your baptism, your graduation and your wedding because he or she wants a seat where he or she can see everything.

A grandparent loves you from when you're a bald baby to a bald father and all the hair in between.

A grandparent will put a sweater on you when she is cold, feed you when she is hungry and put you to bed when she is tired.

A grandparent will brag on you when you get a typing pin that 80 other girls got.

A grandparent will frame a picture of your hand that you traced and put it in her Mediterranean living room.

A grandparent will slip you money just before Mother's Day.

A grandparent will help you with your buttons, your zippers and your shoelaces and not be in any hurry for you to grow up.

When you're a baby, a grandparent will check to see if you are crying when you are sound asleep.

When a grandchild says, "Grandma, how come you didn't have any children?" a grandparent holds back the tears.

Erma Bombeck

Editor's Note: Erma Bombeck is one of America's best-loved writers, even after she passed away in 1996. Most of us consider ourselves fortunate to have an opportunity to read work by Ms. Bombeck. Publisher John McMeel was blessed to have a close friendship with the writer. Mr. McMeel's story appears next.

Solid as a Rock

In the business world, we are taught not to get too close to our business partners. We are told that loving emotions will get in the way of tough contract talks or difficult situations when business partners need to hear the word "no." We are taught to be friendly and cordial, but tough and assertive.

Thank goodness, I don't follow advice very well. Because my friendships with some of my clients, whom we call creators in the syndication business, have been based on a deep and abiding love and respect.

One example was my dear friend Erma Bombeck, the greatest humorist of our time. Universal Press syndicated her column for many years, and our families had more than just a business relationship. She was a dear friend to me and my wife Susan.

Erma Louise (Fiste) Bombeck was born Feb. 21, 1927 in Dayton, Ohio. She got her start as a reporter with the Dayton Journal-Herald, eventually being syndicated in more than 600 newspapers. She was a homemaker who became a nationally known author, speaker, and syndicated columnist. Among her best sellers were "The Grass Is Always Greener Over the Septic Tank" and "When You Look Like Your Passport Photo, It's Time to Go Home." She could make even the hardest of cynics laugh hysterically.

Erma's life was an inspiration to all of us here at

Universal Press Syndicate. We knew this wonderful, vivacious woman who made people laugh every day was someone whose life was not the joke-a-day that one would expect.

Erma's father died when she was only 9 years old. At 20 she was found to have a hereditary kidney disorder that would eventually lead to kidney failure. (Two of her three children have inherited the problem.) In 1991 she had breast cancer and underwent a mastectomy. In 1993 she started four-times-a-day peritoneal dialysis until a kidney transplant April 4 of that year.

On my 60th birthday, Erma, her husband, Bill, my wife, Susan, and I were celebrating at a restaurant in Phoenix when Erma brought out a huge box and put it on the table and said, "John, this is for you." Well the box was heavy, and all I could think about was what a pain it was going to be to check it in at the airport. Erma, as usual, was reading my mind and said, "Don't worry, John, we'll ship it home for you."

I opened the box to find a large, round rock. I thought it was another example of Erma's sense of humor. But when I looked more closely, I noticed the rock was engraved with a word. The word was "laughter."

Erma smiled and said, "Remember, when you find yourself between a rock and a hard place —always laugh."

A few months later, on April 22, 1996 in San Francisco, California, Erma died of kidney disease.

Erma once wrote: "When I stand before God at the end of my life, I would hope that I would not have a single bit of talent left and could say, 'I used everything you gave me.'"

I believe God said back to her: "Job well done."

Many times since then when the day gets chaotic, I find myself looking at that rock and resting my hand upon it, remembering what she said. If I can't bring myself to laugh, I can usually come up with a smile.

Erma Bombeck passed out love and kindness with extreme generosity. I was lucky to be on the receiving end more than once. She will always be a special loved one in my life.

John McMeel

The Communicator

Some men have strange ways to communicate their love. There's bringing flowers home, voluntarily changing the oil in your car and helping with the house cleaning ... occasionally. My youngest son is a baseball radio announcer. He definitely wins my award at communicating his love for me with a series of beautiful and caring events, which he had orchestrated for me, when I flew in to visit him during a game that he was calling.

It started when I arrived at the airport in Florida, and found a uniformed chauffeur waiting for me. He escorted me to a beautiful white, stretched limousine in which I found a dozen yellow roses from my son. The driver said he was taking me to the ballpark and turned on the radio and got the game. I heard my son calling balls and strikes and then he said, "Hi mom. I guess you're on your way to the ballpark about now and I look forward to seeing you and giving you a big hug."

I got to the stadium, where the driver took a Polaroid photo of me leaning against the limo holding my bouquet of roses, with the stadium in the background. I then went up to the broadcast booth where I received a big hug from my son. I will never forget his thoughtfulness and I not only knew he loved me but I felt it as well.

Joan Lucas

Editor's Note: Joan's son, Jim, is currently the play by play radio announcer for the Charleston Riverdogs. When he gave the previous surprise to his mom, Jim was working in Fort Myers, Fla. His long-time broadcast partner, Don Wardlow, is the first blind full-time radio announcer in professional baseball.

The days are too short even for love; how can there be enough time for quarreling?

Margaret Gatty

The Girl Who Said Yes

Deep down I knew she loved me. At least I could have expected as much, considering we had been dating for 18 months (plus the first seven months when we went out solely as "friends" … à la "When Harry Met Sally"). Still, for most guys there is that certain amount of angst that is associated with asking a girl to marry him. "What happens if she says 'no'?" is in the back of the mind for most guys. I guess in my demented way, I thought the easiest way to relieve that pressure would be to ask this girl to marry me … on the radio. Today, with proposals a regular occurrence on stadium JumboTrons around the country, this would be no big deal.

At the time, I was the baseball announcer for Lipscomb University in Nashville, Tenn., meaning I could combine my love of baseball and broadcasting to my love for Libby. The arrangements were perfect. I would be graduating on Saturday, so my family would be in town. Libby was from the Nashville area, so her parents were already there. We had a road game scheduled for Memphis on Friday. Perfect. I set things up with the radio station, the school's Athletics Director, Jonathan Seamon, and with baseball coach, Ken Dugan. Perfect. We had a graduation party on Thursday night, anticipating leaving early the next morning for Memphis. I think everyone at the party that night knew what was going to happen the next day … except Libby. (Although she probably could have guessed from the grapefruit-sized fever blister that had found its way to my bottom lip.)

In my Utopia, Friday was set up like this: my aunt and uncle who live in the Nashville area invited my parents, along with Libby and her parents, out to their house for lunch. They would all be listening to the game on the radio. At a specific moment during the game, I was going to pop the question. Someone was going to be at the radio station, ready for Libby's phone call —hopefully a "yes." Since I was going to be broadcasting the game solo, no one would be around me when I "popped the question." There was one minor problem … rain in Memphis.

The game was postponed until the next day. Graduation day. Do I miss the graduation ceremonies that my parents had waited five years to attend? Do I ask Libby to marry me in some old-fashioned way? Or, do I wait until next season? Believe me, I toyed with a couple of those ideas.

As it turned out, since it was a beautiful Friday, the team decided to practice that afternoon before leaving for Memphis. Coach Dugan agreed to do a "special" 30-minute coach's show. The station had already allotted the time for the game, so it was no sweat to them. Tom Lawrence, who had actually helped me pick out Libby's ring, would be waiting at the station for Libby to call with her answer. And lunch was still being prepared at my relatives' house. Once again, things were back on track. We decided to take the last 10 minutes of the show for THE question.

That first 20 minutes might have been the longest

20 minutes of my life. Finally, the time had arrived. After a commercial break, I started to send out "hellos" to my parents, then I started talking about Libby, and mentioned the fact how we had been "going out for awhile."

"It's about time for you to marry this girl, isn't it?" Dugan quickly quipped. Had I been as smooth as I wanted to be —or thought I was— I would've played off Coach's lead. I didn't. Despite the fact everything was scripted by me, I still stuttered to the point of near-incoherence as I finally got around to popping the question. Then, more bantering between Dugan and me, with his comments such as, "Hold on, Libby; I think you should call me at home tonight at [then gave his home number] before you call the station." And, "Go ahead, Libby and marry the guy. I'm sure you could do a lot worse. At least now we know there'll be an athlete in the family."

My dreams came true ... Libby called in with her "yes"! Again, there's always that doubt for a guy that the girl might surprise him, but the thing that got me the most was after she gave her answer, she ended the call by saying, "I love you, Matt." I was floored.

People usually aren't going to forget the day they got engaged. For me, being surrounded at the exact moment by friends who loved me, and a girl who expressed it on the radio, I will always know that I am loved. If I ever forget, I've always got the tape ... want to listen?

Matt Fulks

The Lesson

A group of us started visiting nursing homes in the late 1970s, sharing newspapers, magazines, candy and ourselves with the residents. It is a give back program that lets both parties get to know each other and learn how our aging friends handle tremendous adversity. Through the years you see so much evidence of love, with residents helping each other in an effort to find ways to conquer the dreary days of loneliness.

While visiting with a 104-year-old, vivacious lady, whose mind was still very much alive, I inquired, "What do you attribute your long and useful life to?"

She simply replied, "I give love; I get love."

Enough said.

Bill Grigsby

Editor's Note: Since 1963, the team's first year in the city, Bill has been a member of the Kansas City Chiefs radio broadcast crew.

The Magical, Loving Cat

Our family has learned that love comes in all shapes and sizes. We discovered a special form of love through our cat, Topaz. Topaz was named for his rich, golden eyes. He came into our lives on a cold, wintry day in February almost nine years ago.

We knew he was a magical cat from the beginning because of the way he entered our lives. He was an abandoned kitten. One day he hovered by my husband's car outside his business all day. Topaz never budged from under the car. There was something about this car he liked, he had made up his mind.

When it came time for Walt to come home, Topaz was still huddling under the car. Walt called home and asked us what we would recommend he do about the cat. Knowing how independent cats are, I knew it would be unlikely for the cat to respond if he was called. Nevertheless, my recommendation was that Walt call the cat and if he came then it was "kismet" and therefore Topaz was meant to be our cat.

Walt got in the car, left his door open and called the cat. Topaz immediately responded by leaping onto Walt's lap where he stayed the whole ride home.

Although we were eager to meet our new cat, we were to discover he was a mangy mess upon his arrival. He had ear mites, fleas and worms, as we were to find out the next day from the vet. He was relegated to the garage on his first night in his new home, much to the disappointment of our three animal loving children.

The next day we took Topaz to the vet's to get "fixed up." It was then that we discovered he was about seven months old and had been fending for himself for a long time. The vet said Topaz had the largest and sharpest canines he had ever seen. We thought it was amazing that he was so friendly and gentle towards us since he had been on his own for so long.

Topaz always preferred the outdoors. He roamed the neighborhood at night. During the day he would come inside to eat, sleep and get "loved-up." Normally he found a quiet corner in the house to curl up and sleep. That was until Miss Cynthia was learning how to crawl. Our daughter Cynthia was born with spina bifida. She didn't naturally learn how to sit up or crawl as other children. She needed help. She needed to be taught. She started receiving physical therapy in our house when she was about seven months old.

Magically, Topaz started appearing at Cynthia's bedroom door whenever the therapist would come. He would stretch out just inside the room, just beyond Cynthia's reach. He would lie quietly, watching. It was as if he knew he was needed. Topaz was very faithful. He would lovingly come to Cynthia's room each and every time the therapist would visit. Each time he would stretch out in front of Cynthia no matter where she was located in her room. Cynthia wanted to touch the cat. She would reach for him frequently, making longing, semi-frustrated noises in her attempts. The therapist came to realize that Topaz could be used as a "carrot" during Cynthia's sessions.

One glorious day, with the videotape rolling, Cynthia scooted forward to touch Topaz! He waited calmly, and stayed put so she could finally reach him. This magical, loving cat purred as she moved to pet him.

Topaz continues to remain near to Cynthia, always ready with a purr of encouragement. Cynthia and Topaz love each other dearly. It is a special form of love.

Sheila Kemper Dietrich

The Meaningful Chase

My grandmother, Inus Marie Holladay, had recently moved to Nashville. MaMa, as she was affectionately called by all 12 of her grandchildren, had moved in 1995 after living all of her previous 84 years in rural West Tennessee. She was battling cancer and moved to Nashville to reside in an assisted living community. At the time most of our family lived in the Nashville area.

My grandfather had died in 1981. MaMa was a resilient woman. Soon after my grandfather's funeral, MaMa returned to her garden to raise her award-winning roses. "Life must go on," she was heard to say. Leaving the community where she had always lived was a hard decision for her, but it was a decision she made on her own.

Soon after she had moved in, my brother and I went to meet her for lunch. We met at her home and walked to the complex's cafeteria. The cafeteria line was short and we each picked up a tray and proceeded through the item-by-item line choosing the Jell-O first and ending with the roll selection.

On the way to our table, she introduced us to some of her new acquaintances. The conversation during that lunch was the standard type of talk with MaMa. "How's your schoolin?" and "Ain't nothin' more important than a good education," were phrases that she commonly used in conversations with her grand-children.

She talked about how she liked her new home and described the life stories of her peers who sat at different tables in the cafeteria. Then she pointed out one of her peers who she called the "Grumbler." She explained that the lady did not want to be in the assisted living community and that she rarely spoke a positive word about anything.

At that point, something happened that neither my brother nor I expected, but something we will never forget. MaMa boiled down her 84 years of life into two commandments to live by. She explained to us that during her life she had learned that money and power were not important. Then she told us that after all of her years on earth, she had learned that life could be boiled down to two things:

1. Always tell the truth
2. Always treat people right

You see, MaMa had experienced a long and successful marriage, been active in her church and in the community, helped run a small business, raised four children, and spent time with 12 grandchildren. She had lived through the Great Depression and World Wars I & II. She had experienced losing my grandfather and living life without him.

What she did that day was instill in my brother and me the important things in life. She told us the key to a happy life and instructed us not to chase the unimportant things in life that would one day be meaningless.

It is amazing that the truths we learn as young children are the truths that are still standing at the end of our time on earth. My brother and I often say that we wish we had had a tape recorder to document our conversation at lunch that day. However, we will always remember the words of wisdom from a life that left a legacy and impacted so many people.

"Always tell the truth and always treat people right."

Kolin Holladay

The best proof of love is trust

Joyce Brothers

The Phantom of My Opera

My husband and I adore each other. It's the second marriage for both of us and we truly appreciate the harmony of our relationship.

One night about three years ago, when Joel couldn't sleep, his creativity took over. He planned my 50th birthday party exactly as he imagined I would like it. During the three years that followed, he built upon and honed his original ideas to create an extraordinary birthday extravaganza for me.

What an act of love it turned out to be. There were two hysterical presentations, one by our blended family of five kids, three spouses plus five of our seven grandchildren (two were less than 1 year old); and the other by my elementary school girlfriends.

The highlight of the party came when my husband, with no previous dance experience, performed the part of the "Phantom of the Opera" with a professional woman ballerina. He had secretly trained with her for three months. Since dancing is my passion, this was his gift of effort and caring just for me.

The masked Phantom surprised everyone, especially me, when he removed his disguise as we danced to our favorite song, "Truly." He then offered his toast of eternal love for his lifetime and beyond, which reflected my own deepest spiritual feelings. My fantastic evening continued and was enjoyed by our friends and family until 2:00 a.m.

Even now, my inner being is still aglow with the excitement and deep meaning of the evening which was one of those "moments" that make for a wonderful life of love and happiness.

Shelley Tauber

Those who love deeply never grow old;
they may die of old age,
but they die young.

Benjamin Franklin

The Pomona Sparrow

In the mid-1960s, I served as a pastor to two small churches. My salary was minimal and our personal budget very tight. From time to time at the point of our deepest financial need, my wife and I would receive a check in the mail for $10 or $20 with a note signed, "The Pomona Sparrow." We always thought it was one of two families who had the wherewithal to make such a gift. On the day we moved from that community in 1967, we received a final piece of mail. In the envelope was a letter that said:

Dear Coopers:

Now that you are leaving, I will find a new person to be a sparrow to.

(Signed by the person)

A most insignificant lady whom we would have least expected ... many teeth missing ... always attending church in her little red hat. To some ... an outcast ... a sparrow. To us ... an Angel bearing great love.

Bud Cooper

The Power of Friendship

Stephanie and Katie became friends in the first grade. It started like all grade school friendships —you come to my house, I'll go to yours. From the beginning, these two were constant friends. Except, of course, for the inevitable period when jealousy and other friendships drew them temporarily apart. But back together they were.

Their personalities have always been tremendously compatible. Stephanie is acquiescent, accepting and consistent; while Katie is effervescent, excited and vocal. As the years moved on, they matured in parallel fashion, becoming fast, best friends. Katie, my daughter, always wanted Stephanie on family vacations. And Stephanie was one of those few friends that we as parents could enjoy for a solid week! So to the mountains skiing, to Florida beaches, and to our lake home, Stephanie came. Through the years, I became, in Stephanie's words, her "second mom."

In the summer of 2000, during a phone conversation with Stephanie's mom, she asked an unusual question. Then, concerned about Stephanie's future and the crowd that she had become attached to in their new school, we both agreed that Stephanie would come to our home if ever it were needed. Her mom expressed how much Stephanie loved us, and how it would ease their concerns if we provided that second safe home … just in case. Without hesitation, my husband and I agreed.

A few months passed and I received a second call

from Stephanie's mom, with a very different tone to it. She had been diagnosed with inoperable cancer. With her typical acceptance of such issues and peace in her heart, she recounted to me the complex and painful treatment that she would go through —from losing her hair to perhaps the final loss of her life and her family. I marveled at her ability to relate this awful situation with the same inner acceptance I have seen in her daughter all these years.

In addition to the medical situation, she asked once again if we would take Stephanie into our home as she and her husband feared he could not provide the woman-to-woman nurturing that Stephanie needed. Again, without hesitation, I said yes.

Now, as she works through her treatment process, knowing that the chances for recovery are slim, our family, with Katie our last child at home, proceeds with mixed emotion. Hoping and praying for a miracle for Stephanie's family, we know also that friendships have a reason and a purpose that exceed our current awareness. We know that our lives might change in the not too-distant future and that our arms might grow for one more. We also know that we are participating in one of life's major lessons. As Stephanie's family reached out to our Katie for so many years, we find it only natural to do the same. And so it goes that love begets love, and friendships create very special families.

Betsy Stewart

I have known many,
liked a few,
Loved one—
Here's to you!

I love you more than yesterday,
less than tomorrow.

If we cannot love unconditionally,
love is already in a critical condition.

Johann Wolfgang Von Goethe

Through the Eyes of a Child

Recently, I have been undergoing a topical chemotherapy for the treatment of skin cancer. My normally pink skin is now an angry red with weeping and crusting as the treatment effectively causes the abnormal cells to dry and fall away.

My grandson, RJ, recently came to visit. When he first saw me and as we talked, I became aware that he couldn't —or wouldn't— look directly at me. Our daughter reminded him to make eye contact as he talked to his grandmother. RJ looked at me painfully and said, "You know, Nanny, red is my favorite color." Touched by his sensitivity, I gathered him into my arms and told him, "I love you."

RJ looked up at me and said, "You still smell like Nanny."

A little afraid of a child's honesty, I asked, "And just what does Nanny smell like?" Without hesitation he replied, "Like a garden."

An uncomfortable situation was suddenly turned into a moment to cherish because of a grandchild's love.

Nancy Poetz

Come live with me, and be my love.
And we will all the pleasures prove,
That valleys, groves, or hills, or fields,
Or woods and sleepy mountains yield.

Christopher Marlowe
"Passionate Shepherd to His love"

To Listen is to Love

I have stayed in touch with a college classmate for over 50 years since our graduation. We live a continent apart and see each other perhaps once every four or five years. He has had a long history of medical problems, arising from parachute landing training during the war.

Recently, he called late at night, his voice full of trouble and desperation. He listed a series of problems: health, his frustration and inability to get acceptable legal help for an invention, trouble with his children —out-of-work, irresponsible son-in-law and a fight with a daughter— and loneliness.

He went on for a half-hour. I listened, murmured a few syllables to indicate I was still there, but offered no advice. When he finished he said, out of the blue, "I love you."

The moral to the story is that just being there is often enough.

Anonymous

Unconditional Love

Years ago, during my first "real" job after college, my grandmother came to stay with me in my 3-floor walk-up apartment in downtown Denver. The apartment was extremely sparse and lacked many of the usual home amenities. However, my grandmother decided it was time to teach me to make her special chicken pot pie (not the baked kind, but the Pennsylvania Dutch-thick, homemade-slabs-of-dough kind). We embarked on a shopping excursion to buy every cooking implement possible, along with a giant cooking pot and many freezer containers. Since I didn't own a car, we set out by bus.

All went well and we found what we needed. Although the chicken really didn't pass her muster, she decided it would have to do. Then our luck turned. It began to rain and the shopping bag became soaked. We got off the bus and stood waiting to cross a four lane city street to get to my apartment building. After waiting for an inordinately long time, we began to hustle across the street. Wouldn't you know it, the bag broke. Stewing pot, utensils, flour, potatoes, onions and chicken went everywhere on the street. I looked at my grandmother and she looked at me and we both dissolved into hysterical laughing. Despite the traffic, we managed to gather everything into our arms, climb the hill to the building, and the stairs to the apartment.

By the end of the afternoon we were exhausted from recurrent giggles, but the apartment smelled of chicken pot pie. I had learned my grandmother's secret —which I still manage to recreate once or twice a year. We had a series of other adventures, but this silly one stayed special to us. I always knew my grandmother loved me absolutely and unconditionally.

Patti Greene

Unexpected

Peggy was expecting our first child, and the house we were building was still far from completion. Of course, the baby arrived right on time but the house was still a month from finishing.

Then, unlike today, new mothers spent a week in the hospital. The day Peg went in to labor, I asked all the workmen to meet with me. We agreed that they would work around the clock to try and complete the job in a week.

A week later, as we left the hospital, I asked Peg if she felt up to dropping by the house and seeing if they were making any progress. Of course, she knew nothing about my arrangement.

We parked in front, and as we reached the front door I said, "At least, I should carry you across the threshold."

The door swung open and she gasped because the house was complete; carpets, furniture, drapes, lamps, the beds made and the nursery welcoming. Everything in place, ready to move in and spend the night.

She looked at me and said, "I love you." She had said it many times before, but somehow, this seemed special.

W. H. Helmerich III

What is Love?

I recently underwent liver transplant surgery. Afterwards, I learned the true definition of love. It is easy to love when all is well, but does "in sickness and in health" include months of care? Does it include changing dressings and giving infusions? Cleaning up surgical oozing? For my husband it did —all the while making multitudinous chores like nothing: The only thing he couldn't mask was his pain at my pain.

What is love?
His hand holding yours for 45 minutes in the middle of the night until the pain lessens.

What is love?
The admonition "don't look so sexy" to me (with three abdominal tubes yet to be removed).

What is love?
Sleeping on the floor and never complaining so I could have the bed to myself.

What is love?
Arranging flowers that I could see from my bed.

What is love?
Dispensing pills even though he knows I hate to be reminded.

What is love?
A sweet kiss ... a heart that cares.

What is love?
My husband Bob ... lover-friend-nurse.

Bobbi Bridge

You're Wonderful!

I grew up as an only child. My father passed away when I was 13. There was never any doubt in my mind that I was loved, and Mother did think I was wonderful until I began seriously dating. It was clear no one I liked would ever please her but as I approached my 25th year, after dating this special person for some two years, marriage vows were exchanged.

My wife did everything she could think of to be helpful, kind and considerate of Mother. Still, my wife felt that no matter what she did, she would never be good enough for me in my mother's eye. I heard the little negative remarks and watched the coldness. Two children blessed this marriage, and while Mother doted on them, my wife continued to struggle to be accepted in her eyes.

Mother died suddenly in my 17th year of marriage, at a time when my career was at its height and there was scarcely enough time for proper burial and mourning, let alone to dispose of household effects. Mother's personal things were put in a large steamer truck and sent to our house to be stored in the basement. We never seemed to have enough time to even sort things through until I retired, nearly 23 years later. As my wife and I looked through the material, we came upon Mother's diary, kept during the years of my dating and up to her death. Entry after entry extolled this wonderful girl that I had found.

Mother recorded each and every one of the kindnesses that my wife had shown to her in the sense of true appreciation. The writings after the children were born extolled her virtues as a young mother, a wife, and the wonderful home that she kept.

With tears streaming down both our checks, we were determined never to make the same mistake, by realizing it is never too soon or too late to say you're wonderful!

Dr. D. Kay Clawson

*Love doesn't make the world go 'round.
Love is what makes the ride worthwhile.*

Franklin P. Jones

You've Got Mail

Mom,

Some little snitch from this leadership class told everyone about my birthday. So I am getting all of these email greetings. Anyway ... I do thank you for life—for staying in bed so I could live and for everything else you have done and given to me!!
I love you.

Susan

Editor's Note: Betty Keim provided us with this e-mail she received from her daughter, Susan Rohrer. Before Susan was born, Betty had a placenta previa and was confined to bed for three months.

Proud Father

I remember the date very well. It was November 25, 1989, just after 1:30 in the afternoon. My first child, a son, had been born. Needless to say, I was beaming with happiness.

After the nurses had measured him, weighed him, and made sure he had all of his fingers and toes, I was finally able to hold him. It was a feeling I had never experienced before, one of total expression. I felt it coming out of every pore of my body. As I looked at him, I felt a total connection. He had been moving and wiggling around with the nurses, but as soon as I held him, he relaxed and started cooing. After a couple of minutes, he grabbed my thumb on my right hand with a very strong grasp and wouldn't let go. From that moment on, he didn't let go until I handed him to my wife, and still, he wouldn't let go. We had to almost pry his hand off my thumb.

"LOVE" is defined in many ways, but to me, this was the first time in my life I had ever felt this kind of attachment and feeling of total expression. For me it was the echelon in my life of what "LOVE" is to me.

Andrew Jacobs

The Stranger

As I stood there watching friends and family pay their respects to my grandfather, one man caught my eye. He had sneaked in, paid his respects, and started to leave. Before he had the chance to slip out unnoticed, I pulled him aside and asked him how he knew my grandfather.

"I knew him in boot camp, when we were in training for the war. I have not seen him since. When I saw his name in the obituaries, I had to come to pay my respects," he replied. He then turned to go but I brought over my father to meet him. My father also asked how this man knew my grandfather. Dad was given the same response. The man then left as fast as he had come.

After the wake, my father and I were talking about this man that we met. We told my grandmother, but she didn't know who it could have been. Nobody knew this man's name, but he knew my grandfather.

This man had not seen my father for 53 years, yet he felt obligated to come to the wake. My grandfather must have done something special to touch this man's heart, and in only the six weeks of boot camp. It is amazing how one man can touch the life of another in such a short time.

Brad Bonney

Love makes time pass—
Time makes love pass.

May we kiss those we please
And please those we kiss.

May we love as long as we live,
and live as long as we love.

John Milton

Ski Run

My wife and I enjoy our many grandchildren, from their homemade cards to their telephone conversations, there is an "I Love You" stuck in there. One memorable vacation we had with the grandchildren was skiing on Mt. Hood and helping them to either learn or improve their skiing. On the last day of our trip, one granddaughter was enjoying her improved skiing. She and her cousin wanted to make "one more run" down a ski slope (it's bad luck to say "the last run"). The girls started down a trail we had skied several times during the daylight; however, it was late in the day. Even though the lights had been turned on the main slopes, the tall pines blocked the light on other trails. They either had to ski in the dark down to the lift, or be rescued from the cold. Luckily, a young female ski patrol on a snow mobile was sweeping the trail. The big thrill for them was riding the snow mobile back up the dark trail with the lights on.

After loading onto the chair lift to make "one more run," our granddaughter felt safe again. Riding the lift, with the lighted ski slopes below us, over the top of some of the pine trees we could see the last rays of the sun setting behind the mountains in the distance. At that moment, our granddaughter leaned over and kissed me on the cheek and said, "I love you O'popa Jer's."

Jerry Fladung

Dad ♡
Thank you for being the best
father I could ever ask for
and ever want. I have
so many wonderful childhood
memories thanks to you.
    I Love You!
                ♡, Nancy

Reflections

Over the years, Marion and I have been richly blessed and it has become a challenge for our children to find the perfect gift for the Holiday Season. As is true with many active families, December is a time of great anticipation, but also a great number of activities competing for time and attention. Our four children told us they had planned a very special evening for us and that our only instructions were to keep the designated evening completely open, and clearer directions would follow.

When the evening arrived they told us to select comfortable clothing. What arrived was all of our children and grandchildren who bid us happy holidays and then yielded the house to a caterer who had prepared our favorite meal with our favorite wine to be enjoyed in the peace and solitude of our own home. We had time to reflect on the outpouring of love from our children and to pause and enjoy the very special relationship that we have had with each other for 45 years. A moment to pause and reflect on the special time of year and the special joys of our shared lives.

Henry W. Bloch

Editor's note: Henry is the Chairman of the Board for H&R Block, Inc.

I love those who can smile in trouble,
who can gather strength from distress,
and grow brave by reflection.

Thomas Paine

Fowl Weather Friends

Migratory waterfowl hunters have three great loves: the opening day of duck season, the outdoors in autumn and enjoyable hunting companions. In fact, the opening day of duck season is of far greater significance to a hunter than Christmas Day or one's own birthday!

A few years ago, opening day was somewhat cool and cloudy, and my two companions in the concrete duck blind were my minister, Reverend Bill, and Patrick, his college son. Patrick and I had dressed appropriately, with good chest waders and hunting coats to give us maximum protection from the elements. Reverend Bill, however, wore only hip boots that came up to just above his knees with a very light, non-waterproof hat, a camouflage jacket and cotton blue jeans.

Soon after we arrived in our duck blind, a light rain began to fall. With the rain, ducks of multiple varieties started to whiz by our blind. As we commenced shooting ducks, the rain became heavier, the temperature fell and the birds became even more plentiful. Patrick and I zipped our protective coats up to our chins and pulled our waterproof hoods over our heads to keep warm and quite dry. Bill, on the other hand, was getting wetter and wetter, and colder and colder.

The ducks continued to fly in, settling in among our decoys in front of the blind, and the hunting was simply unbelievable! We were shooting ducks right and left, feverishly honking our duck calls and retrieving the downed birds at a frantic pace! It was a duck hunter's dream —especially for opening day when hunting is generally slow. Bill's light hat and coat were soaked.

Soon, we had nearly bagged our limit of ducks for the day, but they just kept coming in. By this time, Reverend Bill's pants were completely sodden from his knees to his waist. Rain had plastered his insufficiently light coat to his skin. The plummeting temperature caused him to shiver just slightly. The relentless rain had inundated his glasses. Between the streaking raindrops and the fog of his own breath, he could scarcely see.

Finally, Reverend Bill turned to me and said in a voice that shook with heartfelt sincerity, "Dick, it just doesn't get any better than this."

Dick Bond

Editor's note: Dick is a Kansas State Senator.

Soul Mates

On our wedding bands, we have inscribed the words: "God sent you to me and me to you." We feel that is why we met on June 12, 1987 at 11:30 a.m. Looking back, we truly realize that many circumstances had to be "just right" for us to have met that day nearly 10 years ago.

We were at the Greenbrier Hotel in West Virginia; both there for different reasons. I was there on business and she was there to get away from major responsibilities of the care of two bedfast parents. For the first time in our lives, we were both feeling a little sorry for ourselves. We were both saying, "Please God, help us out." We met because we feel God put us into each other's path that day. (I was scheduled to play tennis but my group was late, and it also began to rain, which caused the match to be canceled. She was walking by the tennis courts but had to seek shelter from the rain.)

So we met, had lunch, talked and then parted. We kept in touch and realized we had found our "soul mates" in each other. We married on December 8, 1989.

We both believe, without a doubt, that God answered our prayers ... and that WE ARE LOVED!

Conrad Hock

If we discovered that we had only five minutes left to say all that we wanted to say, every telephone booth would be occupied by people calling other people to stammer that they loved them.

Christopher Morley

The Gift of Presence

Birthdays have always been important events in our family, and presents are traditionally a big part of the celebration. Usually, family members pool funds and together purchase one great gift for the birthday person.

As my mother's 70th birthday approached, my two brothers and I wrestled with what to give her. This was a milestone birthday and we wanted the gift to be something very, very special. But what?

My parents and one of my brothers live in Wisconsin. My other brother and I live in Kansas City. Since we all have families and hectic schedules, it's a rare treat when we can all be together in the same place. It has only happened once or twice in the past 10 years.

After lots of thought, we decided that Mom's 70th birthday was the perfect time for all of us to get together. We agreed the best gift we could give would be ourselves.

In order to surprise her, my brothers and I made excuses to Mom about where we would be and what we'd be doing that weekend, apologizing for not being able to celebrate with her and Dad in Wisconsin. We assured her that we'd be thinking of her and would certainly call to wish her well on the big day.

When Mom walked into the restaurant on the night of her birthday and saw the whole family there, she was absolutely speechless. She was so excited and delighted to have us all together. The happiness on her face assured us we'd chosen the right present — the gift of our presence truly said, "You are loved!"

Debbie Hagen

Love is the condition in which the happiness of another person is essential to your own.

Robert Heinlein

A Bittersweet Moment

Remembering my father's death in September 1992 brings back bittersweet memories. Beloved by everyone who knew him well, his passing obviously left a void in the lives of his wife, his children and his grandchildren. We were saddened, but we were also comforted by the fact that he had enjoyed more than 87 years of happiness and good health, and that he died peacefully with dignity. What we did not recognize at the time was how many other lives my father had touched.

One unexpected moment that revealed to me how much love my father had inspired occurred at his funeral. As we gathered at the cemetery to lay him to rest, my cousin Stephen approached me to express his condolences. "I will always remember your father fondly," he said. "He was the only adult other than my own parents who loved me and treated me with respect for as long as I can remember. Even as a young child, at a time when other adults hardly noticed me, Uncle Moe talked to me as an equal, the same way he addressed any adult. I will always remember him for that."

It makes me proud to know that the love my father offered his friends and family was so strong and so abiding that it has overcome the sadness at his passing and continues to warm the hearts of those people who knew and loved him.

Carl Schulkin

Love is life.
All, everything that I understand,
I understand only because I love.

Leo Tolstoy

MY FAVORITE TIMES
ARe Being
WITH YOU XOXOXO
You ARe SPECiAL
Be CAUSe You
ARe MY DADDDY
Nicole

New York Mets Kind of Love

The New York Mets baseball team had always been my first love. As a youngster I was thrilled by their improbable "Miracle" championship in 1969. As I moved past my "wonder years," I wondered to myself whether I could share this passion with anyone else, and if anyone could really understand how much the team meant to me.

I started going out with Liz in 1978, a period in which the Mets were playing miserably. They would go on to finish dead last that season. Liz liked baseball, and had occasionally gone to Shea Stadium to root for the Mets, although she wasn't what you would call a rabid fan. We didn't go to any games together that first year, but on the opening day of the 1979 home season, I was to find out how much she loved me.

It was a brutally cold April afternoon at Shea Stadium as the Mets hosted the Montreal Expos. The temperature at game time couldn't have been more than 40 degrees, and in windy Shea Stadium, it felt even colder than that. Although it was their first home game, enthusiasm for the team wasn't at a high level, and only about 10,000 of us were on hand to take in the game. It was a tight game, and the Mets had a chance to win it in the bottom of the ninth inning after the leadoff batter tripled, but they botched a squeeze play and the game went into extra innings. The game remained tied through the 10th, 11th, 12th, and 13th innings. Shea Stadium got colder and colder and the crowd grew smaller and smaller. Finally, Montreal scored, thanks to a dropped fly ball in the 14th inning, and the Mets lost. It was clear that they would go on to finish last again that year.

What was remarkable to me was not once during the marathon game did Liz complain about the less than ideal conditions. While people were leaving the stadium all around us, not once did she suggest we join them. It certainly doesn't say a lot about me that I probably didn't consider how she felt freezing to death watching an early season baseball game that meant a lot more to me than it did to her. If Liz could be understanding enough to put up with lousy weather, even lousier baseball, and an inconsiderate boyfriend, I knew that I was truly loved.

We were married in 1985, and the Mets won the World Series the following year. Liz and I were at Shea the night Mookie Wilson's ground ball sneaked past Bill Buckner as the Mets stayed alive in the unforgettable Series they would win two nights later. We now have two beautiful children, Met fans both. I can point to that freezing afternoon more than 20 years ago as the day I knew I had found someone very special.

Ken Samelson

I Found Love Once

I found love once
Twas not pretend
He was my coach
He is my friend.

Editor's Note: This was the last verse of a poem that legendary UCLA basketball coach John Wooden received from one of his former players.

To Be Understood

hen I married Bev (a widower) he had four children, ages 12, 10, 7 and 4.

Two months after we were married, my sister visited us for a weekend. (She and I have always been close.) After she left, I shed a few tears. Seeing this, Janet, the 4 year old, came up to me and hugged my leg —she couldn't reach higher. She said, "I know why you're crying. Your sister left and you love your sister." (She emphasized the LOVE.)

I was so touched by her understanding and caring.

Margaret Brown

Love conquers all.

Virgil

Roses are red
Violets are blue
You're the best mom
And I love you!
Stephanie S

Love on One's Nightstand

From the time I was old enough to know the difference between a football and a basketball, I've been crazy about sports. Like most boys, I wanted to excel in athletics, but it just wasn't to be. In high school, I went out for basketball all four years and was cut in the first cut each season. I tried track, but others ran the 1/2-mile in about the same time I ran the 1/4-mile. Still, my love for sports grew. As far as competitive sports were concerned, that love was from the vantage point of a spectator —particularly as a spectator when my sons participated.

Years passed and my greatest thrill in sports came when, as a father, I watched my youngest son, Adam, win second place in the 800-meter run at the state track meet. (Incidentally, four years later that highlight was equaled when I watched him finish well up in the field when he ran for Amherst in the same event at the Penn Relays in Philadelphia.)

The morning after Adam won the silver medal, I woke up, glanced at my nightstand and saw an envelope with "Dad" written on the front. I opened it and out came Adam's silver medal with a note that read, "Dad, this is for you. I love you."

Now, years later, when I hear Elton John's "The Last Song," which talks about love between a father and his son, I remember opening that envelope on my nightstand.

Michael Braude

Mom I Love you dad I Love you to
I hav bin hoping that you had a
goud time ate youer anufiresy I Love
you Mom and Dad. Love Lindsay

The Bottle Person

The room where I took clay classes was warm and inviting. As my sisters and I entered, I knew I would have my work cut out for me. My sisters had all made my mother beautiful clay figures for her birthday. As usual, I had nothing. Can't a 7-year-old procrastinate just a little bit?

I had nothing for Mom, but I saw an old soda bottle and proceeded to make a "bottle person." It wasn't that hard. You flatten out some clay, wrap it around the bottle, and decorate it to look like a person. When I was done I gave it to the teacher. The next day I held in my hand one of the most oddly shaped figures I had ever seen. As I watched it sitting next to my sisters' wizard and witch, I slowly felt myself becoming embarrassed about my creation. When it was time for my mother to open her presents, I felt kind of awkward giving it to her (especially after my sisters' masterpieces). But when she saw mine, her face lit up and she said, "I love it." It was the best feeling I had ever known. To this day, that "bottle person" sits in our cabinet for everyone to see, and you know what, I'm not embarrassed anymore.

Adrienne Mielke

My Special Mom

My Mother is the most wonderful Mom in the world. She is as pretty as a Princess. Her favorite - food is Ice cream. I know she is really happy when she gets to play with us. I would not trade my Mom for a frog or a cat.

I love my Mom very much.

Happy Mothers Day!

Ray

Gifts of Love

For many years I have found great joy making gifts for family members and special friends. Christmas and birthday gifts are the ones I take the most delight in giving. When someone gives me something they have made with their own hands, I am deeply touched.

To me, time is the most precious commodity. This was true when my children were young and family demands were awesome. This is true as I age and find my energy level waning, while my family grows in number and interests. Yet I experience profound pleasure piecing an original baby quilt or needle pointing a Christmas stocking for a grandchild or helping my grandchildren make an original Christmas ornament for their parents, other grandparents, aunts and uncles.

When you make something for a particular somebody, you think about them as you work and it seems to me you sew in or glue or cut in many loving thoughts, memories, hopes, and caring wishes while you work. My children have certainly observed this feeling of mine. From time to time, they have surprised and delighted me with handmade gifts of their own. A beautifully, embroidered poem hangs framed on my wall and a darling quilted "Welcome" pillow decorates my bedroom chair.

When I turned the big 60, my children and their spouses joined my husband and me to celebrate. They brought gifts of love, which truly blew me away. They know me very well and they honored me by putting a great deal of time, thought, and creativity into expressing their love. Their gifts ranged from a board game handcrafted with photos of me through the years (a personalized kind of "Sorry"); to two picture frames handcrafted from old wood collected in a Colorado forest, with photos of my daughter and son-in-law which I had begged for; to a personalized 45-minute "This is Your Life" video tape. Last, but not least, each couple arrived with their favorite recipes and rotated preparing and serving exotic dinners that equaled those of 4-star restaurants around the world. All of the gifts they gave me were truly original, from the heart, and deeply cherished.

I was truly blown away and deeply, deeply touched by the time, thought, creativity, and personal understanding and caring that went into each gift so generously presented to me and for me. I felt I had died and gone to heaven. That time in heaven, surrounded by those I love so much, remains a part of me —inside me— forever.

Susanne Christopher Shutz

Above the Arctic Circle

The year was 1978. My wife, Joan, and I walked across the Arctic National Wildlife Refuge, the northernmost part of eastern Alaska, hundreds of miles above the Arctic Circle.

It was a rugged trip. We were out 17 days with a guide, walking across stark land seldom seen by humans. We followed animal trails made by such incredible creatures as caribou, bear, elk, mountain goats and bighorn sheep. The weather was cold and damp. Mosquitoes in the evening were thick.

On the morning of our seventh day, we finished breakfast, packed our tent, food and other gear, checked the compass, put on our packs and headed out. We walked on hummocks all day. (A hummock is a tuft of earth and grass about six to eight inches in diameter, surrounded by water.) Each time we stepped on a hummock, the leg had to be tightened to assure that our foot would not slip, possibly causing a fall. The difficulty of staying erect was compounded by the weight of our packs. Joan was carrying more than 40 pounds, while I had more than 60 pounds.

By the end of that afternoon, we had been walking on hummocks all day. The guide selected a bare knoll to pitch our tents for the night. I stood behind Joan, took hold of her pack, and as she unbuckled her waistband and eased out of the shoulder straps, I lowered her pack. She crossed her feet and sank to the ground, weeping. She was exhausted. After I got a drink of water and a bite of food for her, Joan took a short 20-minute rest, and was then on her feet helping to prepare supper.

In the barren land above the Arctic Circle, we found out how much we needed each other. Out of that need grew an even greater respect for each other. Out of that respect grew a deeper love.

More than 20 years later, after 52 years of marriage, we are convinced that our trek across the tundra of northern Alaska was a major factor in creating a love for each other that today is stronger than ever.

Bert Berkley

The heart that loves is always young.

Unknown

*Love is when you are willing
to give of yourself endlessly
to make someone else happy
and to ensure their well-being.
It makes you feel euphoric.*

Arthel Neville

A Loving Tradition

As I rocked my grandson to sleep, it was quiet except for the creaking noises of the rocking chair and the distant chatter of his parents and grandpa visiting downstairs. I had read him a book and was now singing softly to him a song that I knew so well that my mind could drift.

As I sat and rocked, feeling the warmth and softness that is only true of a sleepy baby, I thought of having rocked his father in that same way, singing the same song — "... and the green grass grew all around, all around, and the green grass grew all around ..."

Somehow I was then transported to a time many, many years ago when I was being rocked to my mother's singing the same songs she always sang as I was nearing sleep.

My thoughts came back to the present and I realized that the sweet child in my lap was sleeping soundly. I sat for a bit, just enjoying the moment and reflecting the comfort that this loving tradition has carried from one generation to the next.

Reluctantly, I put him in his crib, covered him, tucked in his teddy bear, and went to join his parents and grandpa, with my mind still wrapped in the serenity which that song and those memories had brought.

Bev Menninger

It Started with an Ice Water ...

My love started when I was a first year camper in Boy Scouts in the late 1920s. I used to go out with the mail truck to pick up the mail at a local corner. It was sort of a roadside pickup station. On one trip I noticed a girl standing in front of a cottage. I waved and she waved back. She wanted to know if I wanted some ice water. It was a blistering hot day, so I said yes. Her mother, who was standing nearby, thought, "Oh boy, here we go; another puppy love situation."

I saw the girl many times that summer and in succeeding summers, as I attended camp as a camper, then as a member of the camp's staff, until I had to finally go away to college. When I had completed a couple of years of college, my father decided it was time for me to go to work. I got a job with a personal finance company in Greenwich, Conn. Lo and behold, the girl I had gotten ice water from as a first-year Boy Scout, lived in White Plains, which is not too far away. I decided to call and make a date with her. We dated frequently until I decided it was probably time for us to get married. We were wed on October 4, 1940. We have been together ever since.

Cliff Gruber

I COULD NOT STAND IT WITHOUT YOU DAD I ♥ U LeAnn 6 1990

Dear Gramma
I Like the cradle
and the Baby step
I Like the Books
you gave us
thank you
Love
Laura

P.S. I LOVE YOU

Dimensions of Love

I have come to believe that my love for the persons I know (especially my wife) makes perfect sense. That is to say I understand my heart's conviction, the soul connection, so my commitment to them is filled with logic and purpose. Even though that joyous entanglement is more than words can describe, somehow it makes sense. However, I am overwhelmed, feel a sense of the sacred dimension in all things, touch an element of the miraculous not only in my loving but most especially in my being loved.

Love is the part of our lives that is more than logic. That experience, not only more than words, quite literally, defies any clear, sufficient and rational explanations. For here I am with all my foibles, flaws, inconsistencies, weaknesses, and still this other person sees in me and connects me with more than I can comprehend. Yes, to love is wonderful, but to be loved is a gift of God.

Rabbi Michael Zedek

A Game of Jacks

My stomach churned with anxiety during the endless games of jacks my dad and I played on the cold, hard, black and white speckled linoleum floor during my first few years of elementary school. No one else's kitchen in our neighborhood had such a smooth floor, perfectly suited to jacks-playing, my father wryly noted, as if he was a salesman peddling snake oil. I was so lucky, he assured me, that we could sit for hours in the evenings, he and I, practicing, practicing, practicing this game I yearned to learn.

He was right, of course. But back in the mid-1950's, "Father Knows Best" was only meaningful to me as my favorite television show. You see, playing the game itself was not stressful. The emotional turmoil occurred in my facing this unspeakable truth: I simply could not master the game of jacks, the game that was essential to master if I wanted to play with my neighbors in the "jacks marathons" they held each day after school. Not being able to play jacks at the tender age of 6 and 7 and 8 made me an outcast, an outsider, a misfit.

Pessimistic, frustrated, impatient. I embodied these three character traits until my dad's pure love smoothed their rough edges often enough with jokes, hugs and his own personal tricks of the trade to turn them into tenacity, humor, and most of all, optimism, as we practiced. My dad led me to believe that I could get that "eye-hand coordination thing together." I learned from his soothing, daily doses of love that a positive attitude is priceless in growing success. I discovered that the adage, "If at first you don't succeed, try, try again" is fact, not fiction, if you want to reach a goal.

I became the person I am today—in relationships, in work, in play—in part, because of what happened on that kitchen floor: I knew that I was loved. My dad demonstrated that believing in someone creates miracles, a chain of miracles. His kindness was unequivocally contagious as it became the guiding principle in the way I treated myself, my peers, my friends ... particularly when they were struggling. I knew I was loved because he was consistent in his message of support—hour after hour, day after day, week after week on that cold, hard linoleum—and asked for nothing but love in return. He received it, as well as gave it away, every day of his short life.

Decades later, the memory of his love is still a bright candle of encouragement and support whenever a proverbial "game of jacks" darkens my door and stands in the way of making my dreams come true.

Barbara C. Unell

Editor's Note: Barbara C. Unell is the co-author of the recently published book, "The 8 Seasons of Parenthood" (Times Books/Crown). The previous story was taken from a book that she is currently writing on the subject of kindness.

Grandpa's Bragging Rights

Our granddaughter, Meredith, knew she was adopted and wanted to know who her real parents were. She asked us over and over again. Then she stopped for a while. Later, she asked again. When asked if it bothered her, she replied, "I am glad I was adopted, because that way I got Grandpa." That showed real love. Needless to say, her grandpa told the story over and over again.

Helen Jane Uhlmann

Hey, Mom

Have a great time this weekend. I love you bunches + I'll be thinking about you the whole time.
♡ Katelyn ♡ xoxoxo

P.S. I will miss you a ton!

Remember _my_ dog Toby?
Thanks for taking care of him
when I didn't.

Memories in Bloom

My uncle was a well-known gardener who loved flowers and had a beautiful yard full of them. He also planted gardens in different spots throughout our community, creating splashes of beauty everywhere.

His mother had been an excellent gardener, and he told stories of how she taught him to grow and cherish flowers. Our children were devoted to my uncle and especially loved this story ... when he was small, my uncle and his mother planted a forsythia bush and together enjoyed watching it grow and bloom each spring. His mother remarked that when she died, he should think of her in the springtime, as the forsythia bloomed. My uncle passed this lovely tradition on to our children, asking that they think of him each spring when they saw the forsythia in bloom.

My uncle is gone now; and, though more than 70 years old, the forsythia bush still flowers each spring. Our children remember my uncle with love and think of him often, but never more poignantly than when the forsythia blooms.

Yes, the remembrance of love can be sparked by many images recurring blossoms seem particularly sentimental. I guess you could call it "love in bloom."

Paul Uhlmann III

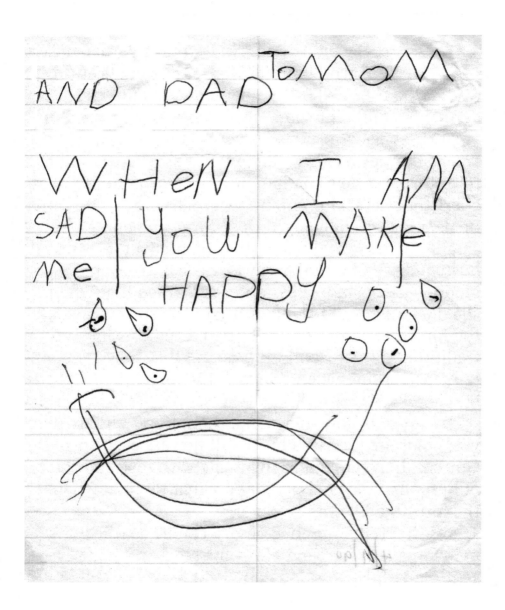

ToMoM
AND DAD

WHeN I AM
SAD YoU MAKe
me HAPPY

For Better or For Worse

In June of 1994, my husband, John, and I were involved in a head-on collision with another car going 55 miles an hour. By the grace of God, the other driver and we survived. The other driver was not seriously injured, which was a miracle. John had a fractured sternum and I fractured an ankle and had severe neck abrasions with a significantly swollen carotid artery. An ambulance had to take me to the local hospital. I was in the hospital several days and, upon being released, I found myself completely incapacitated.

Our marriage vows of 35 years stating, "for better or worse" were definitely tested as my husband literally nursed me back to health. He bathed me, dressed me, came home from work to feed me, fixed meals and completely cared for all my needs.

I thought how lucky I was to be married to someone who, without a word, showed me how much he loved me by completely taking my life into his. Without a thought to himself, he cheered me up and cared beyond belief. I have never felt so loved and protected in my life. The love he showed me allowed my recovery to be significantly faster. I cherish the love that was unspoken but shown to me during this period.

This is the way we believe life should be. It is a blessing when our beliefs become reality.

Bobbi Marks

Prescription for Love

In December of 1992, we received a call from neighbors of my widowed aunt in San Diego, Calif., saying that she was very ill and in Balboa Naval Hospital. After calling the hospital and talking with physicians and corpsmen, my husband and I made reservations to fly to California the next day. We called the hospital and again talked to my aunt's doctor, who agreed that we should come, but advised us that we may not make it in time, as there was NO hope. Later that afternoon, it dawned on us that we should not arrive as a surprise. This time when we called we talked to a young corpsman named Chris and asked him to please tell Aunt Sis that we were on our way. I had not seen her since 1956 (36 years) and my husband had never met her. We talked on the phone monthly but had never been to the West Coast to visit her.

We got to the hospital the next evening not knowing what might have transpired. As instructed on the phone before left home, we went to the Chaplain's office. He was waiting and immediately took us up to I.C.U. Aunt Sis was weak but awake and coherent, and glad to see us. We stayed six days and watched her improve daily. She was in a regular room when we had to fly back home to Norfolk, Virginia.

The corpsman told us that when he told Aunt Sis, "Your niece and her husband are coming out to see you tomorrow," her statement was, "Chris, that's wonderful but you have to help me hang in here until they arrive. I've got to see those kids." She was 84 years old. I was 55, but I was 19 the last time I saw her, so "kids" it was.

The corpsman, Chaplain and doctors said her making it was truly unexpected, but they thought having our visit to look forward to (being a widow with no children or other family), she gave it all she had and made it.

I really think love was a big part of her recovery.

Beth Bernard

Knowledge is gained by learning;
trust by doubt;
skill by practice; and love by love

Thomas Szasz

Commitment & Acceptance

When we hear more and more stories about abused children, it makes us want to stand on a rooftop and yell, "How could you?"

We feel so grateful to have had the enormous blanket of love from our parents, our children and, with luck, our grandchildren. There is no gift more worthy than unconditional, unjudgmented love. We always felt —and hoped our children felt— that they were loved no matter what grades they got, where they went to college, who they married. (Fortunately, we love their spouses and their families —a great bonus.)

It is total commitment and acceptance of each other —be it a mate, a parent, a child or grandchild, or a friend— that is the real meaning of love. That's how we know we are loved.

Bob & Betty Slegman

Dear Mommy,

On mother's day, we don't do anything special to let you know why we are celebrating mothers and we should. It's not very common for a mother to volunteer herself to PTA or other things, but you did. You took a large piece of your time and dedicated it to helping other people and even better, children. I get so many compliments from friends and teachers recognizing your efforts to make things look thier best. It makes me feel special and happy that I have a mom like you! Thanks for being such an amazing mom!!

Love Hannah

An Introduction to Love

I was abandoned by my birth parents in a small town named Moosejaw in Saskatchewan, Canada. The good Lord sent two elderly people, Mr. and Mrs. Fulton Linkletter, to my rescue, and I was introduced to the meaning of the word "love" by their care and comforting protection. They were childless, in their late fifties and poor in the sense of worldly possessions. But the love they gave me in the next 18 years was beyond belief. We were poor in the true sense of the word, and moved often to small houses in the low rent sections of San Diego, Calif. I will always be grateful for the love of the Linkletter family.

Art Linkletter

Editor's Note: Art is a famed television show host and author.

HAPPY
BIRTHDAY
DAD!

Liebchen

After 35 years, there is no longer a dachshund dog at my house. First there was Brunhilde, then Friede, and for the last 17 years, Liebchen. My two grandsons remind me that it doesn't seem like home without a dog. We are understandably sad, but there are treasured memories like her last summer vacation.

Although she was very frail, deaf and nearly blind, this devoted companion was a wonderful passenger on our 600-mile drive to Colorado. I believe she enjoyed her last two weeks of life in the cool of the mountains at our log cabin. Her big German shepherd friend, Jackie, visited her. They had hiked many miles together in past summers.

My grandsons arrived at the cabin a week after she died. They had been devoted buddies, sharing hugs and kisses and years of play. Eight-year-old Patrick loved to cuddle with Liebchen in her rocking chair or curl up beside her in her bed, or cover up with a blanket. The frailties of old age hadn't diminished the love and attention. She seemed more precious to us.

In her memory, the boys collected white rocks and made a cross. Ten-year-old John carved her name on a stick from an aspen tree. It was made into a cross. Wild flowers were planted close by. Our memorial garden was the beginning of healing.

Patrick, in confidence, told me he lit a candle at church when word was received of her death. We hugged, overwhelmed by the love and loss of our faithful friend. Certainly Liebchen lived her life as she was named, lover.

Ann McAdam

Children need love, especially when they don't deserve it.

Harold Hulbert

Lucky Me and Mr. B

My principal, Mr. B, is one great guy.
Let me tell you the reasons why.
My principal, Mr. B is very nice to me.
He makes me happy when I am sad.
He makes me glad when I am mad.
His trust in God is no mistake.
He cries in chapel when he
feels so great.

Soft and gentle is his voice when
discipline becomes his choice.

He is so tall
Compared to me who is so small.
When I hear the door opening
And I hear his keys jingling

I better be in fear?
'Cause Mr.B is near?
No need to fear!
I quickly know when he is there.
When I see his shiny gray hair.
One final fact I think you should know
Is how Mr.B let his mustache go!
In a pep assembly it was shaved
Because of 3200 dollars families gave.
Mr.B's heart is full of love
Like that given from God above.
I'm glad to go to a Lutheran school.
Where I can live by God's rule.
As you can see Mr.B is one great guy.
And now you know the reasons why.

Melinda Hope

It's a shame so many people do not say "I love you" to their own parents, children, relatives and friends. The words give such warm feelings. One is never too young to understand love. Babies know when they are loved. What happens in later life? Why is it that we do not continue this loving, cuddling practice when children get older?

Melinda Hope, my only granddaughter, knew the words "I love you" when she was 1 year old. While visiting us one morning, I said, "I love you Melinda Hope," to which she replied, "I *ove* you too." This made my day and gave me a moment to remember forever.

In today's world one cannot give too much love. We should pass it around — it's free and easy to do. Many of my business associates and friends exchange the word "love" freely. If everyone would love one another more, we would be living in a better world. After all, God made people in his own image and has instructed us to love one another. The more you try loving others, the easier it becomes. Choose someone today that you really care about, and say to them, "I love you." You'll be surprised ... it's contagious. You will help make this a better place to live.

Thomas E. Beal

A Rainbow of Love

When my 93-year-old mother passed away, planning the funeral service was not particularly depressing. In fact, my wife made most of the arrangements, while I accepted condolences from friends and loved ones. I did not look forward to the service or the family luncheon that was to follow. I really just wanted to get the whole thing behind me.

After the funeral and luncheon, the immediate family sat in the living room reviewing the day's activities. I expected depression to set in, but instead I was dwelling on several poignant things that had unfolded —especially kindnesses from my immediate family.

My 8-year-old granddaughter, upon learning of "Mima's" death, called me within minutes. "I feel so sorry for you guys," she said with the compassion of a mature adult. At the funeral she had moved from the pew behind me to sit next to me. During the service she reached over to hold my hand and give it comforting squeezes.

My 18-year-old granddaughter called several times at my office to say hello and tell me that she loved me. My children, in a conversation with my sister, mentioned that they worried about not paying enough attention to me.

It should not have come as a surprise that people would express condolences, and it did not. What did surprise me was the unique, indescribable effect of these kindnesses. The sadness of my mother's passing had provided an unexpected and deeply touching experience, a rainbow, I will never forget.

Arnold Eversull

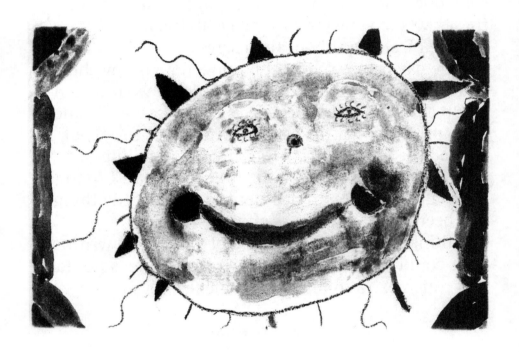

The Note

Love comes in many ways. Sometimes it is so subtle you don't even realize it is there. Other times love stands out, like if someone just told you that they loved you. Both of these ways of showing love make all the people involved feel good about themselves.

One day before school, I found a note in my shoe. I was surprised by the note and wondered what was in it. On the front of this note was the message, "Do not open until you get to school." When I got to school, I opened the letter. It was from my mom, telling me how proud she was of me. I felt good all day. I thought it was great that Mom had noticed some of the things I had been doing with extra effort.

I think it is cool that a piece of paper with writing on it could impact how someone feels. It does not take that much extra to make someone feel loved.

Kyle Harrison

I love my
baby brother.
Dion

The Perfect Spot

Several years ago, while vacationing in Colorado, I decided to put the Accardo family on top ... of a mountain. The long hike to the top would be a lot of fun and bring us together. Our two sons, Jon and Chris, were 8 and 9 years old. They were enthusiastic and more than willing to carry a heavy load on their backs up the mountain —the spirit was willing but the bodies were small.

My wife, Aggie, was reluctant and dubious about the whole experience. Her idea of camping out is a hotel room with only one bathroom. At any rate, the boys and I created enough excitement to persuade Aggie to join in.

Since this was our first family overnight hiking excursion, we all proceeded to shop for the proper tent, padding, stove, pots and pans, dried food, water bottles, apples and granola bars to eat on the way, sandwiches, gas for the fire, flashlights, matches, Boy Scout knives, fishing gear, sun glasses and, of course, a hammock for relaxing on the way up. We also took rain gear in the unlikely event of bad weather, and extra shoes for the kids should their feet get wet. The list goes on and on.

Finally, the morning of our big trip arrived. Three out of the four of us were very excited. We started before dawn on a crystal clear day in Vail. Everyone's backpack was full, including Aggie's, and she knew it was too late to back out of the trip. We climbed up the hill that quickly turned into a mountain. About an hour into the hike, the kids were complaining that their packs were too heavy, so we started lightening their load. Guess who got to help carry their load? The trail got thin and then disappeared. Aggie was convinced we were lost. However, the great outdoorsmen (the boys and I) knew the trail would appear again some place … we hoped.

After about nine hours of rigorous climbing, storms started moving in and the likelihood of our starlit dinner of fresh trout on top of the mountain was beginning to disappear. We finally made it to the top when the icy, cold rain was coming down in buckets, along with an occasional flash of lightening that kept us moving quickly to erect the tent. Wet and cold, we finally made it into the tent and the four of us cuddled, hungry, but too tired to eat.

Aggie, who hardly slept at all, was very upset the next morning (boiling mad might be a better description). She proceeded to whisper harshly to me, "I'm cold, still wet from last night and tired. You pushed me into this trip —don't ever ask me to do it again. It may be the worst experience I've ever had." After half an hour of chilling silence, Jon woke up, peered out through the slit in the tent. We had set up the tent overlooking a beautiful blue lake, and the sky was an intense blue. Jon and Chris gave their mom a big hug and said, "Mom, isn't this the best thing you have ever done in your life? I love you."

Nate Accardo

Bunny Love

In the spring of 1937, following a harsh winter on our Marion County farm in eastern Missouri, I had the measles with complications. As an only child of a couple whom would have loved a large family and who knew there would be no more children, my illness caused great concern.

I was moved into my parents' bed because their room was the warmest in our drafty old farmhouse. Since many people at that time believed that light could hurt the eyesight of children with measles, the shades in the bedroom were always drawn. I spent hour after hour hardly knowing, or caring, if it was night or day.

One Saturday evening, my father went to town to buy groceries. After a while our party-line telephone rang. I heard Mama say, "In the dime store window?" Then the awful question that every farm wife of the Depression era would have asked, "How much is it?"

A pause, and then my mother said, "A dollar? We can't spend a dollar on a stuffed Easter bunny. You may think he looks like he wants to come with you, but that rabbit had better find another home." The conversation ended, and I drifted back to sleep.

The next morning I awoke early. My folks came into the room at dawn and propped me up in bed. Dad raised the shade slightly, and there, sitting just outside the window in Mama's window box, was a gorgeous stuffed yellow Easter rabbit, with a huge basket of brightly colored eggs my mother had dyed the night before. I had never had a stuffed toy from a store before. This rabbit even squeaked when you squeezed him. Despite my illness, I was ecstatic. I thought that rabbit was the finest creature anywhere.

Later, I heard my father ask my mother why she had dyed the Easter eggs for the rabbit's big basket before he had come home from town. "Because," Mama said, "I KNEW you were going to buy that rabbit."

A puppy has since chewed one ear of that old rabbit, and though the ear has been replaced, it does not quite match the original. The squeaker wore out long ago. But that bunny continues to be a part of my Easter decorations every year, reminding me of my great fortune in having received the wondrous gifts that only loving parents can provide.

Anita B. Gorman

God created man because he loves stories.

Elie Wiesel

The Doctor Who Cried

In 1948, Dr. Paul Brand, an orthopedic surgeon, and his wife went to India as young missionaries. He remembers with sadness and a sense of failure the treatment of one of his first patients, Anne, the infant daughter of missionary parents who traveled a long distance to see him. Anne was vomiting and was severely dehydrated. Her intestines seemed to be completely blocked, and Dr. Brand operated immediately. He removed a section of the impacted and gangrenous bowel. The surgery went well, and Anne was returned to her parents who were staying nearby.

One week later, they were back. The surgical wound was odorous and leaking. It was as if no healing had taken place. Dr. Brand was perplexed and embarrassed. In the second surgical procedure, he stitched with meticulous and fine stitches.

Those were the first in a series of surgeries on Anne. In spite of blood transfusions, hydration, skin flaps, and numerous other procedures, the surgical wound never showed the slightest indication of healing. Anne died.

Dr. Brand was as devastated as Anne's parents were. He cried in grief and helplessness at the funeral. He suspected no doctor could have saved her, but he felt like a total failure.

Thirty years later, after Dr. Brand and his wife had moved back to Louisiana, he received an invitation to speak at a church in Kentucky that was celebrating its

100th anniversary. Anne's father was the pastor of the church.

Dr. Brand was surprised and puzzled by the invitation, but he accepted. His feelings of inadequacy and guilt returned. He wondered how these people, whom he had let down and about whom he had cared so deeply, would receive him.

When Otto Artopoeus introduced Dr. Brand from the pulpit, his words were like this: "I want to introduce Dr. Paul Brand, our family's good friend. I have told all of you about him. He is the doctor who cried when our baby died."

There is a song title, "What's Love Got to Do with It?" This story seems to answer that question.

Becky Benson

Editor's Note: Dr. Paul Brand told the previous story while speaking at a meeting of The American Society of Surgery for the Hand. Becky Benson, whose husband, Dr. William P. Benson, is a long-time friend of Dr. Brand, shared the story with the permission of Dr. Brand.

The Most Glorious Sight in the World

Once upon a time in a small town, a young girl saw the most glorious sight in the world. Hanging on a hook in the hardware store window, was the most beautiful silver sled she had ever seen. World War II was over and airplane metal could now be put into use for civilian purposes.

Every week, she and her mother would walk to the neighborhood movie theater and they would always pass the hardware store window. Every week the girl and her mother would stop and stare at the bright, shiny sled hanging on the hook. The small child would gaze in wonder, never dreaming of asking her mother or grandfather, with whom she lived, for such an expensive item.

It was four weeks before Christmas and the weather was cold and blustery. Routinely the mother and child braved the temperatures on their weekly trek to the movie house. One day they passed the hardware store and the silver sled was gone. The hook was empty! The little girl could feel the warm salt tears running down her cold, red cheeks. Someone had bought the sled!

Christmas morning came and the bright lights of the Christmas tree illuminated the dark house. The small girl slowly came down the staircase, and lo and behold, she saw a miracle. Under the tree, with a big red bow attached, was the most glorious sight in the world … the shiny, silver sled!! The owner of the hardware store let the mother pay for the sled in small sums, when she was able.

Decades have gone by, the mother has since passed away and the small girl is now a grandmother. Times have changed, but never will the grandmother forget her mother's love and devotion and sacrifice in making that Christmas long, long ago, one that will always be remembered.

Linda Hall

The Sosland Camera

In 1977, I was 16 and very excited to be a part of a group of high school students making a pilgrimage to Israel. I was one of the few boys on the trip who had never had a Bar Mitzvah. One of my friends on the trip, Josh Sosland, convinced and inspired me that it was possible to accomplish in Israel what I had not done when I was 13 years old.

Josh coached and taught me Torah blessings and I was Bar Mitzvah'd on a beautiful Sabbath morning at the Western Wall in Jerusalem with several of my very closest friends. It was one of the greatest and most meaningful days of my life.

Shortly after we returned to the United States, Josh came by my house with what he described as a belated present. He bestowed a German Contaflex camera manufactured in the 1930's. The story behind the camera has become the gift itself. In 1937, when my grandparents fled Nazi Germany, they brought with them five cameras they had hoped to sell to raise money to help begin a new life in America.

Josh's grandfather, David Sosland, had purchased from my grandfather, one of the cameras 40 years previous to the gift of the Bar Mitzvah that Josh had given me.

Jim Gerson

A Mom Is Like a Flower

A mom is like a flower
On a sunny summer day.
You'd pick her in a minute
If you could have your way.
A mom is like the sunshine;
She warms your heart each day
And makes you feel like smiling.
It's just her special way
Of saying that she loves you,
The way that mothers do.
A mom is very special.
That's why you love her, too.

Love Ryan

Love For a Lifetime

My story surrounds the meeting of my wife, Linda. What I have to say involves many incidents of love and caring. Throughout our relationship, there were notes stuck on my mirror, put in my calendar book, slipped onto the seat of my car, attached to a card in my suitcase, and many other places that are far too numerous to be mentioned. The message on the notes was always "I Love You."

In October of 1994, I received word that I had melanoma cancer. When I told her the news, the first words from my future wife were, "Skip, I shall love you forever, and will be with you no matter what happens. I will take care of you whether we ever get married or not." For the first year, my cancer did not spread and I felt fine, taking experimental treatments at the John Wayne Cancer Institute in California. During that first year, in July of 1995 at a restaurant in Paris, we became engaged. Three weeks before our wedding that December, I found that my cancer had metastasized and we had to move our wedding up so I could enter surgery immediately.

Since our wedding on December 10, 1995, my wife, Linda, has been a friend, partner, lover, and advocate every step of the way. Her love has been unconditional and beyond comprehension with every moment being special. She has seen me in my best and worst moments with a caring in her eyes that keeps me going. How could I be so fortunate to have someone who gives unselfishly and who could have taken another path, especially after my cancer?

Our love has grown deeper every day, and we have more love in the time that we have been together than most people have in a lifetime.

Skip Nottberg

Editor's Note: Skip passed away since writing this story.

Gravitation cannot be held responsible for people falling in love.

Albert Einstein

Prince

My father was dying. The last days of his brutal battle with cancer had arrived and there was nothing more to do or say. He lay very quietly in his bed at his home and was pain free, the nurse saw to that. He knew that I was there, on the bed next to him, inches away. All I had to offer was my presence.

My family would be coming soon, driving to share this painful time with me and so I waited for their arrival. I heard them enter the house and I knew they would soon be coming down the hallway to find a way to let me know with their eyes, their hugs, their tears, that they were aching for me. There were no words that could match the poignancy of the moment, so my family huddled in awkward silence. After a while, my husband and children kissed me and murmured some loving words to my father before they left the room, knowing that I would not be leaving my position and sensing that I wanted the privacy of these final hours. They were reluctant to leave but did so to honor my need to stay connected to my father's fragile breathing.

Prince refused to leave. Prince, my beloved dog of 12 years, a small black & brown terrier, knew exactly what he was going to do. He jumped up on the bed and planted his body next to mine, curving every part of his frame to match the contours of my side. It was probably a thought that had passed the mind of everyone in my family but the mattress could not have handled another person, much less four!

Humans have so many ways to express their love for each other. Animals are more limited in their options but Prince found a way, the only way, to say, "I love you."

SuEllen Fried

Sisterly Love

My husband and I had recently taken our 3-year-old daughter, Shannon, to her first wedding. Afterwards, in response to one of her many questions, we explained that you get married when you find someone that you love. Shannon immediately responded that she would marry Erin, her 1-year-old sister, because, "I really love her!" We were very touched not only by her innocence, but by her devotion to her sister.

Julie Doherty

I did not know I loved you until I heard myself telling so, for one instance I thought, Good God, what have I said? And then I knew it was true.

Bertrand Russell

Sisters

When Piper, the younger of our two daughters was born, she was 10 weeks premature, weighing only 3 pounds, 2 ounces. While she spent the first eight weeks of her life in an incubator at the hospital, she was visited many times by her 3-year-old sister, Lauren, who could only peer at her through a large glass window. So, it was an exciting day for us all when little "Sessa" came home from the hospital. Lauren slept on the floor under her baby sister's crib that night, and the next night, and the next. Finally, we put a bed in Piper's room for Lauren, who had pretty much already moved into her sister's room.

That first year was a rough one, with Piper needing constant attention while crying almost continuously around the clock. After her first birthday, it was as if we finally had a newborn baby that slept for four hours each night. By the time Piper was 3, our nights became more normal. Morning after morning, I would walk into the bedroom and find two smiling faces looking up at me, both girls in Piper's crib because Lauren had climbed up to be with her little sister.

Shortly thereafter, Lauren moved back into her own bedroom. We never discussed it or questioned her about it —it just happened. One day her grandmother finally asked, "Lauren, why did you decide to move back into your own room?" Lauren's answer was simply, "Because Piper doesn't need me anymore."

None of us had realized the love and understanding between these two little girls, and the responsibility one of them had accepted for the other. The thought of it still brings tears to my eyes and is one of the sweetest memories of my girls. We'll never know how much strength this bond might have given to our little Piper to help her to survive … we'll never know for sure, the true power of love.

Kathy Rainen

Let's drink to love,
Which is nothing—
Unless it's divided by two.

Love and you shall be loved.
All love is mathematically just,
As much as the two sides
of an algebraic equation.

Ralph Waldo Emerson

Let Yourself Be Loved

He was a keen-witted, athletic young man of 19 when he was struck down by polio in August, 1951. In a single 24-hour period he lost the use of all four limbs for a lifetime.

When tragedy of this nature occurs, the oft-repeated query is, "Why did God allow this to happen?" Though it is supremely presumptuous to assume that one speaks for God, many years spent observing the subsequent life of this unfortunate quadriplegic generates the following opinion: His affliction caused many people to become better human beings than they would have been without him, beginning with his parents who had to care for him unceasingly for many years; to his brother, who abandoned a somewhat hedonistic lifestyle to assume the care burden when his parents no longer could; to three young nephews, who learned to perform many small acts of kindness, cheerfully; and to hundreds of people, mostly nameless, who helped lift, or push, or open a door, when asked.

Surprisingly, however, perhaps an even greater blessing arising out of such adversity is the enforced opportunity for introspection. For the quadriplegic this resulted in a re-assessment of how love should be dealt with. He opined that, typically, most people treat love as a kind of commodity to be disbursed, a variation of, "It is better to give than to receive."

One of the reasons for this popular position is that it is easier to give love than to accept it graciously. Many times the love recipient feels uncomfortable or awkward when it is proffered. His sheer physical condition forced the quadriplegic to become adept at accepting love in an appreciative manner.

He summarized his findings in an address to his college classmates at their silver anniversary reunion:

> "The Lord gives, and the Lord takes away. Blessed be the name of the Lord. For the Lord then gives again, and what he gives is the love of others, to make up what is lacking. Fate left me poor. Love made me rich.
>
> "What I have learned, what I continue to learn daily, is that there is only one way to put Humpty Dumpty together again: Let yourself be loved. Now, 'Let yourself be loved' may not sound terribly profound. But it must be heavy, because it took me all these years to figure it out."

And then in the year of his death he penned a thank you note to the anonymous donor who contributed $1 million to establish a chair in English Literature in his name:

> "And if there has been any life taught to accept the unmerited, immeasurable, unimaginable, it is mine. So, let it happen, and I will trust future generations to recognize the fathomless humility of your giving, in naming the Chair not for yourself or your family, not even for a sainted teacher or counselor, but for a

person with no claim on your affection. I ask only one recompense: When it comes your time, let yourself be loved, in whatever God pleases."

John M. Jenks

Who, being loved, is poor?

Oscar Wilde

Yes, I Am Loved®

The space that follows is, perhaps, the most special part of your book. While thousands of copies were circulated, this is where your copy becomes unique and special. Whether this book becomes a keepsake or a gift, this is the spot where your I Am Loved story can be shared. Use this space to share, communicate and document the power that is I Am Loved.

I AM LOVED

Share Your Story!

As one of the common themes of I Am Loved® suggests, love is always best when it's shared. If you have a story, poem, quote or "refrigerator art" you would like to submit for consideration in future I Am Loved® books, please feel free to send it to us at:

I Am Loved
Addax Publishing Group, Inc.
8643 Hauser Drive
Suite 235
Lenexa, Kansas 66215
FAX: 913/438-2079
email: addax1@addaxpublishing.com

Attention Schools and Businesses:
I Am Loved® books are available at quantity discounts with bulk purchase for education, business or sales promotional use. For information, please write to:

Special Sales Department
Addax Publishing Group, Inc.
8643 Hauser Drive
Suite 235
Lenexa, Kansas 66215